HOW COYOTE
STOLE THE SUN

The myth, the music,
and other features
of the Yokuts culture

The cover design is from a Yokuts rock painting found in the foothills east of Porterville. It depicts Coyote in the act of stealing the sun, a direct pictorial reference to an ancient Indian myth.

(Permission To use the rock painting design of Coyote stealing the sun was granted by the Council of the Tule River Reservation. Nicola Larson, Chairman)

A myth is a traditional narrative.

Something of the Yokuts voice

has survived translation

and will be waiting in book and video

for Yokuts descendents

and to those among us

who treasure the myths of the ancient folk.

How Coyote Stole the Sun

The Myth, the Music
and Other Features
of the Yokuts Culture

TABLE OF CONTENTS

ILLUSTRATIONS

**COMMITTEE FOR THE PRODUCTION
OF VIDEOTAPE AND BOOK**

"HOW COYOTE STOLE THE SUN"

Bill Seaberg, Associate Dean
Learning Resources Center, Fresno City College

Don Wren
Instructor of Anthropology and Archaeology
Fresno City College

Evon Cody
Past President, Kings County Historical Society

James Leonard
Kings County Historical Society

Robert Painter
Former Assistant Superintendent, Kings County Schools

Dr. Richard Keeling, Formerly with Department of Musicology
University of California, Los Angeles, California

Script for the Video is based on notes taken by
John P. Harrington, Smithsonian Scholar
as told by Tom Atwell, Yokuts Indian, in 1916

Project Director, Marjorie W. Cummins

ACKNOWLEDGEMENTS

Funding
Planning Grant and Grant from the California Council for the Humanities and additional Grant from the Kings County Arts Council

Challenge Match Funds from the Following:
Kings County Historical Society
Advisory Committee of the Kings County Museum
and
AAUW Hanford-Lemoore Branch

Book and Video Production
Produced with the facilities of the Fresno City College
Learning Resources Center, Bill Seaberg, Director
Editing and Graphics for book by Darlene Anderson
Kathleen Vander Meer editorial and writing assistance
Miscellaneous Sketches by Sam Peña
Dust Jacket for book by Bob Marcellus

Video Producer, Terry Taplin of Nevada City, California
Assisted by Larry Gonzales, Fresno City College
also produced with the aid of the facilities of
the Unicorn Co. and Tony Shepherd Co.

A Special Thank you to
Dr. William Simmons, Chairman, Anthropology Deptartment,
University of California, Berkeley
for his helpful critique of the video.

Sabobas Basket
Ethel Delecci, Clovis, California

Yokuts Indians Participating in the Video
Brown Wilson   Paula and Robert Jeff
Rosy Ignacio   Diana and Manuel Thomas
Josephina Martinez

PREFACE

Both this book and the videotape by the same name were produced with some of the facilities of Fresno City College. The California Council for the Humanities and the Kings County Arts Council provided grants for both. Challenge-match funds were contributed by the Kings County Historical Society, the Kings County Museum Advisory Committee and the Hanford-Lemoore Branch of the American Association of University Women.

The book provides additional information and background to the video. It helps the viewer fit the ancient Yokuts tale of How Coyote Stole the Sun into the larger picture of the history and the culture of the people whose myth it was.

This includes history and early development of the San Joaquin Valley, the role of mythology, songs and basketry in the Yokuts culture, and the crumbling of that culture with the coming of the white man.

Both the video and book were released in 1992 to the county superintendents of schools, county libraries and county museums in the eight counties of the lower San Joaquin Valley. Copies are available for sale.

FOREWORD

Like the lives, stories, and events it records, this book too has its history. It began many years ago when, in the 1930s, I became acquainted with a group of Indians, both children and adults, who lived at the Santa Rosa Rancheria in Kings County, south of Lemoore. They were members of the Yokuts tribe and the sub-tribe called Tachi.

The Yokuts tribe occupied the floor of the San Joaquin Valley and the eastern foothills in the early days. It was divided into tribelets. Each had its own territory and spoke its own dialect of the Yokuts language. Professor Alfred F. Kroeber from the University of California identified at least 50 of these tribelets when he came into the valley in 1903 and commenced gathering information for his monumental work, *Handbook of the Indians of California.*

The Santa Rosa Rancheria was established by the federal government for the Tachis in 1921. It lies about 7 miles south of the city of Lemoore in Kings County, or about 40 miles south of Fresno. The 170-acre site lies near what was once the old Tachi-Yokuts village of Wai-u (Wai-oo). The Tachis comprise one of the few active Native-American groups in the San Joaquin Valley today.

As a music consultant for Kings County Schools in 1938, I became interested in these Tachi Indians. Their one-room school was located on the Rancheria. After completing scheduled meetings to other schools, I would often return to the Kings County Library and read what the librarian brought me about the Yokuts: Kroeber's *Handbook of the Indians of California* and Latta's *Little Journeys in the San Joaquin* (some of which was later incorporated into his *Handbook of the Yokuts Indians*).

xiii

One day, out at the Indian school, I asked the class if they had any musical instruments. I knew they did not have drums[1], but I thought perhaps they had a flute. There was a moment of silence.

Then a bright boy said, "We got sticks." They described "clapsticks," pictures of which I had seen in Kroeber's book. We called them "split stick rattles."

My next visit to the Indian School was a momentous occasion. The older Indians and parents came to the school with their clapsticks and sang some of their songs for the teacher and me. The children took some chairs outside where it was pleasant in the early spring sunshine. As they sang, more of their families came, making an ever-widening circle. We watched and listened. It was a rare experience, hearing the ancient folk songs sung by these charming, happy people. This was a different world, a timeless world. They were having a good time singing their own old songs, recalling good times, and laughing together. None of them had any work to do that day. It had been raining for a few days, and the spring season work had not yet begun.

After they sang each song, I asked them the name of the song, what the words were, and what they meant. The leader was Clarence Atwell. He repeated the words for me and helped me spell them. In all of the elementary schools of Kings County, in fact in all counties of California at that time, children studied about Indians. The group thought that school children might enjoy listening to their songs too, and Clarence indicated that he would be willing to dance for them. When he heard that the Indians were singing again, a local man volunteered to record

---

[1] Yokuts had a foot drum. It was made of a hollow log, split lengthwise and laid over a slight depression in the ground concave side down. The Indian stood on the convex side of the log and pounded out the rhythm with a long stick.

their songs. He had a recording machine that could cut a phonograph record. He made an appointment with the Indians, and we all went to the school one evening and made the recording. I spent part of my summer transcribing those ten songs onto staff paper. This I did by playing the record over and over; they are indelible in my mind, even today.

At the time that I transcribed the songs into music notation, I had no idea that others had been to the Tachis and collected songs; but in my later reading, I kept finding references to ethnographers who had visited the Tachis and recorded their songs.

Why were so many scholars interested in Tachi-Yokuts songs? The answer is, it was somewhat a matter of geography.

A Matter of Geography

In the five Tachi villages at the north and northwest shore of Tulare Lake there were perhaps a thousand Indians. (More of this and their leader Tinsin, later.)

To the east of the villages was a treeless plain, land no one wanted because after the spring rains there was no water there. The promising green grass of March and April turned brown and dried under the fierce summer heat until the fall. Later, the fog settled in, cloaking the plain in dreary cold for weeks and weeks. Only the sagebrush survived.

To the west of this group of Tachi villages was another treeless plain, desert-like as the one to the east, beautiful in the early spring, but soon burned by the relentless heat. It too was a waterless plain. Indians could travel through that plain to the hills, the "west-side" hills, where antelope abounded. They went there to take advantage of sunny days in the winter when fog continually hampered life at the lake.

The five villages were quite isolated by these two desertlike stretches of land and so the Indians were able to pursue their lives somewhat as they had before the white man came. They had their medicine man, their calendar of seasonal events, their songs, and their mourning gatherings. Their relatively isolated culture was being partially preserved, and for this reason they attracted the interest of many collectors of Indian materials and students of Indian culture.

In 1978, I went to Santa Cruz to see Frank Latta to ask his permission to use the story he had collected from an informer named Yoimut. Yoimut's story was needed for the book I was writing about the Tachi-Yokuts.[1]

When he saw the material I had, he granted the permission, and he suggested that I go to Washington D. C. to see the notes collected by John P. Harrington. Everyone knew about Harrington, that he had visited Indians everywhere and that he had amassed a good deal of material but had confided his information to no one. He had preceded Latta, and the latter wanted to know what the Harrington notes contained. To further impress upon me that I should go to Washington, Latta paced the floor, saying over and over, "You should go to Washington and see the notes of John P. Harrington." I had the idea that he would have gone himself but was prevented by a heart condition. His wife and a student were present and looked furtively at each other fearing that he was so excited that it would bring on another heart attack.

I did go to Washington (in 1980), and the very first set of notes I found were those of Carobeth Harrington's transcription of Harrington's meeting with Old Tom Atwell, complete with a beginning and ending which looked as though it was ready to send off to the publisher. I compared it with the notes that

---

[1] Marjorie W. Cummins, *The Tachi-Yokuts, Their Lives, Songs, and Stories,* Fresno: Pioneer Publishing Co., 1978.

Harrington had made on the spot (which were made in pencil and very difficult to decipher), and satisfied myself that the information given by Old Tom in the manuscript was identical with what Carobeth[1] had written, and read her transcription into my recorder. I had seen how the story could be presented to the public in an interesting way...and so, with a longer and more informative introduction, I have written the myth for this book.

---

[1] Carobeth Harrington was J.P. Harrington's wife. She was with him at the Tachi-Yokuts rancheria in 1916 and later lived in a cabin in the Tejon area. Being pregnant and feeling neglected, she had him drive her to Southern California where her parents lived and afterwards divorced him. She soon took an assignment to investigate the Chemehuevis, a tribe of Southern California, where she met and married a Chemehuevi named George Laird. She has written a book, *Encounter with an Angry God.*

CHAPTER I

INTRODUCTION
TO THE MYTH

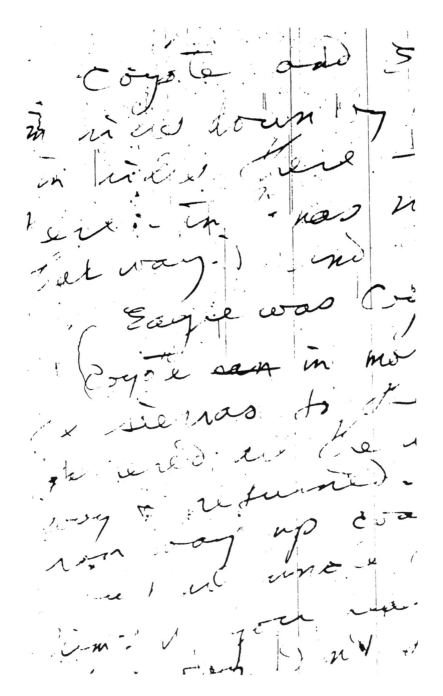

Introduction to the Myth
Tachi Tom and A.J. Atwell

Tulare Lake was once the second largest lake in the state of California; only Lake Tahoe was larger. It was shaped like a saucer—shallow and almost round, 40 miles long and 40 miles wide. It was surrounded by tules so thick and strong that one could not easily find a way to the water. Indians knew the places of access. A woman would wade out into it 100 feet or so, the water not coming above her waist. Turning her basket upside down and lowering it to the depth where her ankles were, she would turn the basket over and bring it up to the surface full of clear, cool water.

There were islands—sometimes three or four, sometimes one or two, depending on the amount of water and the strength of the flow. There were descriptive names on the earliest maps, like Bird Island and Skull Island. There was to be another name, Atwell's Island, on later maps. The islands rose from the water only about 12 feet, but there were trees on them — good-sized willows. They could not be seen from Waiu, the Indian village at the north end of the lake, except when pointed out by a very experienced person on a very clear day — and then only to someone with good eyesight and a strong imagination.

A man from Visalia rode horseback over to Tulare Lake one day in the late 1850s and stopped at the Tachi village of Waiu. Sometimes, whites needing someone to do farm work would come

3

to the Indians for help. But this time the visitor wanted information. He asked if anyone lived on those islands out in the lake.

The man from Visalia was A.J. Atwell, a young lawyer who came to that little settlement in the late 1850s. He set up a law practice and in 1861 married the prettiest girl in town. Finding that the islands were uninhabited, Atwell bought some hogs. With the help of an Indian boy about 12 years old called Tachi Tom, he ferried the hogs across to the islands on tule rafts. The experiment did not work. The hogs ate the mussels that grew along the shores of the islands and it gave them a fishy taste. Atwell and Tom had to remove the hogs and put cattle there instead.

The Tachi boy later went to live at the Atwell residence in Visalia. There he found a stable, horses, and a buggy to take care of, and there were messages to be carried to businesses down town. The A.J. Atwell house was an adobe on South Bridge Street, just a few blocks south of Main Street.

His was to be a life of divided loyalties—loyalties to his Indian friends and loyalties to the Atwell family with whom he lived. One of a kind is always lonely. We can imagine that he very gradually became alienated from his Indian friends as visits to the Tachi Rancheria became less and less frequent.

The Atwells had a family of nine children, and later there were many grandchildren. Atwell served the community in many ways during his career not only as lawyer but also, at various times, as owner of the first steamboat on Tulare Lake, as owner of a lumber mill in the mountains, as owner of the town paper and as legislator, superintendent of schools, and judge.

Tom must have learned that there were frequently constraints in his communications with this other culture—words he must not say and things he must not do. He must accept the criteria his employer required, and then he would be rewarded with trust and responsibilities. As an added bonus, Tom was taught to speak good English. He didn't always use the right form of a verb, but he would

4

be told in a kindly way. "Tom, we don't say he done, we say he did."
"Yes, ma'am," he would reply. Mrs. Atwell could not let her
children learn to speak poor English; Tom must set a good example.
(Later he could be more open with the scientists who came to learn
about the Yokuts culture.)

Tom continued staying with the Atwells, running errands and
doing odd jobs. As the family increased, we can imagine that he
sometimes took care of the young Atwells while Mrs. Atwell was
away, and it is not hard to imagine that he would gather the children
together and tell a few Indian stories — about when Coyote and his
six little boys set fire to the tules or about a man who lived at a
rancheria at the bottom of the lake. He would tell how the animals
climbed up the straight, black trails converging at the top of old
Tutshau, the high mountain, and went into a hole at the top there,
appearing again in the morning at the bottom of the lake.

Tom was forbidden to tell the stories that were bloody, that
used what whites thought were obscene words, or that named
certain parts of the body (Indians called a spade a spade).

But sometimes at night, perhaps, Tom would tell the children
a very special story when they were in their beds in the little adobe
house. Then, in the flickering light of a candle, or the steadier light
of a kerosene lamp, . . . Tom would tell a myth— a myth about
animals.

When he took the part of Eagle in the story Tom would look
very sober and speak in a very low voice, "If you hear anything up
that way," he'd say, hunching his shoulders to make himself look
large like a roosting eagle, "don't touch it."

And, when he took the part of Coyote answering the chief's
question, "Where do you come from?" Tom would reply in a very
high voice, "Come from south. There are lots of people down
there." He would pretend innocence, speaking overly nice while
telling Coyote's lie, for in truth there were only two—Eagle and
Coyote.

In due time, Tom took a wife[1] and had three children of his own. They probably lived in one of the Indian villages near Visalia. Maybe once in a while, for special celebrations, Tom and his family would go to Waiu. Tom branched out doing farm work for neighboring farmers, but he still kept in touch with the Atwell family. And, when he was in his late sixties, Old Tom was taken out to the lake and given a cabin there on a bit of property owned by the Atwells. (The Atwells hoped to sell some of this land to the Indians.)[2]

Always, Tom tried to keep his ties to his own culture. He remembered with nostalgia the myths and tales told around the fire at night when he was a child, the mothers and fathers and children snuggled close to keep warm. He knew that it was customary that the sacred myths be told only at night in the winter, and that any violation of that rule could cause the teller of the myth to be bitten by a rattlesnake.[3] Likewise, not paying attention or going to sleep could cause a child to become hunchback—a dreadful fate!! Reciting the myths had brought the members of the tribe together and had strengthened their common heritage.

Tom remembered the time eleven years before when Professor Alfred L. Kroeber had visited the rancheria and had asked him all kinds of questions about Yokuts Indian ways. "Tachi Tom.[4]

---

[1] His wife's name was Carrie Pohot.

[2] Brown Wilson said that Tom sold only one piece to an Indian and that afterwards the priest bought it. He said the state later bought it from the priest and added it to the rancheria.

[3] Tom may have had to get permission from the chief of the tribe to tell this tale to Harrington in the daytime.

[4] The use of the name, Atwell, seems to have been discouraged. In place of the name, Tom Atwell, he was Tachi Tom. They preferred the name Tachi Tom so there would be no question of paternity. By the time Kroeber appeared, A. J. Atwell was deceased, and probably both the name Tom Atwell and Tachi Tom were used.

supplied most of the information in the chapters about Yokuts," was written in Kroeber's[1] notes.

Kroeber, from the University of California at Berkeley, was in the habit of going by train to a railroad station near his objective and renting a buggy for transportation to the locations of the various Indian tribelets.[2] It is likely that he hired Tom Atwell to drive him to the places in the southern part of the San Joaquin Valley where Indian villages would be found. With Tom as interpreter, he would gather much information, as Tom could speak both English and Yokuts.

Tom wished desperately to interest the young fellows at the rancheria in the stories he was ready to tell; unfortunately, he only evoked their ridicule. At one time, he came to Brown Wilson, his nephew, and cried at this disappointment. This part of the culture, which he held so dear, was dying. Now, young Indians could light candles at night and do something else with their evenings; fascination with their myths was, in the words of Brown Wilson, "Now, no more."

Fortunately for us, there were interested listeners—the anthropologists—who asked their questions and wrote down the myths and tales they heard, word for word. To these men Tom Atwell proved an invaluable resource. Professor Kroeber heard and recorded many features of Yokuts culture; and because of Tom, J.P. Harrington, the talented and tireless recorder of Indian lore, was able to bring us the interesting myth that we have here: "How Coyote Stole the Sun." It was an important myth and a popular one of the Southern Valley Yokuts, a myth that Kroeber regretted not having obtained on his visit in 1903.

---

[1] See Kroeber's notes in the Bancroft Library, Berkeley, CA.

[2] Kroeber coined the word, "tribelet" when he visited the Yokuts in 1903. Kroeber estimated that there were upwards of 40 Yokuts tribelets at the time of his visit, with the possibility of 60 before the advent of the white people in 1772.

Old Tom and J.P. Harrington in 1916

An important event was about to occur: the telling of an old, old tale, a myth which has been told in the Indian tribe for many generations—for hundreds of years—or more. This day, Tachi Tom[1] had promised to tell a myth.

John P. Harrington left his little Ford roadster at the rancheria and walked leisurely in the direction of Tom's cabin. The khaki pants and old wool jacket he was wearing were comfortable clothes for his work "in the field". At 30, his dark brown hair was beginning to thin, the result of his incessant drive toward more contacts and more information from the native people that still retained much of their old culture. The Smithsonian Institution in Washington, D.C. had sponsored some of his work, and now they had put him on the payroll as an ethnologist. He was to save what he could of the cultures, especially the languages, of the North American Indians.

He could see Tom pumping water outside his cabin, across the road from the rancheria. Harrington and his wife had been at the Tachi-Yokuts Rancheria south of Lemoore for about a week. The chief had offered an empty cabin which some of the women then cleaned. Every morning Harrington would knock at the doors of neighboring cabins to visit awhile or to help with the chores.[2]

The centuries of Indian culture in his background were still a part of Tachi Tom. Now nearly 70 years of age, he would find enjoyment in thinking back to the stories and beliefs of his youth.

---

[1] It was said that Tom Atwell was a Wowol Indian born on an island in Tulare Lake. When the Indians left the island, Tom and his sister went to live with the Tachis.

[2] Information given by Brown Wilson, Old Tom's nephew, in 1987.

"Morning, Tom," said Harrington. "Well, it's a little cold this morning."

Harrington sat down on the wooden bench under the tree near Tom's cabin. "Oh, the cold soon ends," replied Tom, and having filled his water bucket Tom eased into an old chair there. Harrington was a clever interviewer. He decided to take a different tack, one that would give him some real information. Later the words and symbols of his scribbled notes would be transcribed by Harrington's wife Carobeth, and written out in legible longhand.

"Do other Indians come down here and dance sometimes?" he asked.

"Yeah, Indians in wintertime come down. Dance all night."

"Where do they go then?" asked Harrington.

"In the summertime, they go back down there," replied Tom. ("Tom confuses the meaning of down and up," Harrington thought to himself.)

Harrington changed the subject. "Is this your place?" he asked.

"Oh, no," replied Tom, "My place is way back of Poso Teneja." And he turned his head in the direction of the Coalinga foothills.

"What's that like?" asked the visitor.

"It's like a rock, a person," Tom said wistfully, "and can still talk." And he turned and looked at Harrington to see if Harrington would believe him. "I was going to take information there," he continued, "but never did."

Harrington was taking notes of everything that Old Tom said; and Tom, reassured by Harrington's silence, went on.

"My uncle also wanted to take me down to Devil's Ranch. There's a little lake there, too," he mused, "I never heard the name. That lake has now shut up." He cast a sideways glance at the listener to see if he would understand. "Doesn't like modern times," Tom said.

Tom was thinking back to his youth, sorting out beliefs long held. The information came in pieces, dredged up from the past, freed at last from the constraints of the other culture to which he had been bound.

9

"The little turtles lived on the north side of the pond there, and the wind lived on the south side," he said, and he nodded his head for emphasis.

Tom was warming to his subject now, and he spoke with more assurance as he saw that Harrington was not challenging these beliefs.

"Turtles were adult—never grew." Tom's voice was stronger and ceased to tremble. "The pelicans are there, though. This is near the high mountain north of the four peaks." And Tom looked in the direction of old Tutschau as though getting re-acquainted with an old friend.

* * * * * * * * *

There was a bit of silence. Tom cleared his throat and we can surmise that he said, "This is from the old, old times, when animals were men like we are."

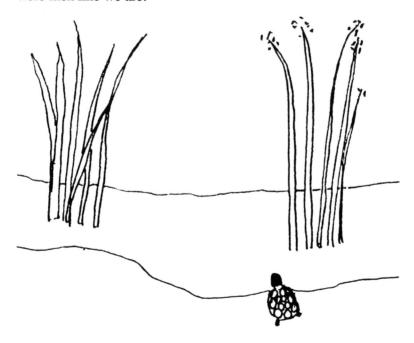

CHAPTER II

THE MYTH ITSELF:
HOW COYOTE
STOLE THE SUN

Coyote and Eagle li[illegible]
ved down by Baker[illegible]
lived there and [illegible]
it [illegible] it was never [illegible]
t way. [illegible]

Eagle was Coyote's uncle
Coyote ~~saw~~ in morning [illegible]
he was to the north
[illegible] the wood up
[illegible] returned. Then [illegible]
[illegible] up coast [illegible]
[illegible] up [illegible] the Eagle
[illegible] uncle [illegible]
[illegible]
[illegible]

THE MYTH ITSELF:
How Coyote Stole the Sun

Coyote and Eagle lived down by Bakersfield, in the hills there. They had a sweathouse. Their house was inside the solid rock. Eagle was Coyote's uncle. Coyote in the morning ran up the Sierras to the north and gathered all the wood. Then he was going to run up the coast side.

His uncle said, "If you hear anything up that way, don't touch it."

Coyote ran up the Coast Range about sundown and came to the place in back of Tutschau where the sun was hung up—in a fetah tree—right in the middle of a clearing. All kinds of animals were dancing around in the open.

Coyote said, "What is this?" He lay down close and heard the dancing and singing.

He went back that same night and told his uncle, "I heard singing down that way the other side of the hill."

Eagle said, "They're people; don't touch it. Don't close in up there, you'll get killed."

But Coyote wanted to see how the sun was tied to the place. He went back the next night. He still didn't know how the sun was tied to the fetah tree. He lay there close until near morning, and then he heard some people say, "The wood is nearly gone."

Coyote said, "What'll I do? I still don't know how it is tied. Well, I'll bring the wood."

He went back to Eagle. When they had eaten breakfast, uncle told him, "Don't go close to it."

Coyote gathered wood for that night and brought it from way down where Eagle was. When the animals came for dancing, they found the wood already there.

They said, "Here's lots of wood." Then Coyote made himself like wood and the people threw him into the fire. But he was like green wood in the middle of the fire and did not burn. The people said, "Oh, it's green," and they threw him out again. The next night

Coyote came back again—a little early that time. Some people saw him and took him to their chief. The chief said, "Where do you come from?"

"Come from south," said Coyote, "There are lots of people down there." But, in truth, there were only two, Eagle and Coyote.

The people said, "Do you know how to sing?"

"Yes, I know all kinds of singing," said Coyote. So Coyote sang with them. By that time, he knew the songs they had there.

"Is this the way they sing?" said the people.

"Yes," said Coyote, "The south people sing that way too."

When he had finished singing, he returned to Eagle and told his uncle all about it. "That fire there hanging on the tree, that's the sun." That's the way he told him.

Uncle said, "That's no fire, that is the sun."

"It is loose, not tight. Can't we get it?" said Coyote, "Pretty soon will be changing."

"Can you get it?" said Eagle.

"Yes, it's easy. I'll get it," said Coyote.

"Can you run?"

"Certainly, I make good runner." That's the way he told him. "If you're a good runner, all right—if not, that's the last we're hearing of it," said the uncle. Uncle told him to go and see if he could pull up a mulberry tree. One has to pull it straight up without breaking it off. If it breaks off—no good.

Coyote went out a little and pulled one up, but it broke off. Uncle told him to go way up north along the Sierra. Coyote did so, and the tree did not break off.

Then he fixed sharp sticks by using the root end of the tree. The uncle told him to shoot the fire where the animals were dancing, and that would make the fire burn way up high. Coyote did so.

The fire blazed up and became so bright that the people there could see nothing for awhile. Then Coyote sprang up, seized the sun, put it in his sen (his net-sack), fastened this securely to his belt, and ran toward the lake.

When the fire burned down and the people saw their sun was gone, they sent out their best runners to catch him. They shouted, "Catch him, kill him!"

Some went to the east side, and some went to the west side of the lake; and they all went down to the south where Coyote ran. Pretty soon, Coyote got close to home. He was tired. Coyote said, "Clut, open," and his house opened and shut up again with Coyote safe inside.

The people came there and crowded all around the house. Some said to open it. And others said, "Oh, let him go. We can do nothing with him. This is a rock house."

Coyote peeked out of the door and said, "You all go back home (motion with hand). You are all old fellows. You can't run at all. You go back (motion with hand). Go back. You have no sun." And the people went back home.

When all this was happening, the Uncle was gone. Soon he came walking along slowly (gestures of walking with hands and arms), and he came home. Coyote called out, "We got the fire! Oh, I'm tired," he said. "I pretty near got caught."

Then Coyote got his breakfast—stayed there all day. Uncle told him, "Tomorrow you can put the sun way up" (gesture to the east).

The next morning when he was getting breakfast, Uncle warned, "Don't put it close in there, you'll burn everything. You'll burn."

So that's the way he told him. Coyote took the sun to the high mountain up east of here. They call that lake Tú-lo-ni.

He took a bunch of tule, put it way up high, and put the sun on top of it. He came running back. But Uncle yelled at him as he came near, "What's the matter—it's getting hot. I told you to take it WAY OFF!"

Coyote went back and moved it. He put it WAY OFF. When Coyote came again, Uncle said, "Did you put it WAY OFF?"

"I put it way off, WAY OFF," Coyote said.

Then the sun came out and was not much hot. Coyote said, "Is it too hot?"

"No, it's all right," Uncle said. "It's all right now."

* * * * * * * * *

"There is a place back of Tutshau where there is a circle of standing rocks. (Tom made a circle with his two arms). When the people lost the sun, they changed to stone. Have Crow on one side and have Coyote on the other side. Crow people are on one side, and Coyote people are on other side." (Gestures with arms.)

"Some of their face painting can still be seen. My uncle said he would take me up there, but I never went to the place. A trail goes up there into the mountains."

"Gut Ho, the raven, those are all his hills, (gesture) west side hills. Those big crows are there at Devil's Ranch and everywhere there now. And the eastern hills were the hills of Limik, that black hawk (falcon)."

* * * * * * * * *

Tom was beginning to tire. He told fragments of stories.

"But the people down there have no fire now. The chief sent the people all around the country. He told them, 'That is your place. Put a chief for them there.' (Tom was stopping, searching his memory.) And he sent another kind of people....to live in a slough there."

"They used to dance all night....swimming all night, that was their dancing. They were watersnake people." (Tom nodded his head. His voice was getting softer. It was as though he was talking to himself.)

"Then one year ago, the boys went down there....and that fellow, Wa-ti-o-ti, came out. He wanted to tie their wagon. From there, I don't know. He wanted to stop them" . . . .

"That's all I know....I guess."

Harrington wrote in his notes, "Wandering talk, no more information at that time."

16

Tom leaned back in his chair, his head resting against the faded material, and remained quiet for a while. Harrington knew when to keep silent. He wrote a few notes on his paper. A red-winged blackbird flew into the branches above, twirped, and then made off again.

Harrington rose, put his face close to Old Tom's and said, "Shall I get you a drink of water?" Tom was startled out of his reverie.

"Oh, oh, no. I'm all right. Went to sleep," he said.

"I'll see you tomorrow, or next day," said Harrington, "Whenever you're ready."

burrow owl

17

HOW COYOTE STOLE THE SUN

CHAPTER III

PRESERVERS
OF THE MYTH

HOW COYOTE STOLE THE SUN

PRESERVERS OF THE MYTH

The myth "HOW COYOTE STOLE THE SUN" was saved: first in the notes of J.P. Harrington in 1916 and now in the video produced in conjunction with this book (in a form that Tachi Tom had never imagined, even in his wildest dreams). The video, telling the myth in motion pictures, in color, and with an audio of native songs and oral language, gives us a re-created myth in another art form.

How old are the myths? They are probably hundreds or possibly thousands of years old. As time went on, perhaps they were changed somewhat. As different personalities became the teller, the individual's stamp would be left on the myth. They might be added to, borrowed, forgotten, lost through death, or invented anew.

Professional preservers of Yokuts myths have included A.L. Kroeber, 1903; J.P. Harrington, 1916; Frank Latta, 1925; and Anna Gayton, 1925. The above dates are approximately when they started collecting data on the Yokuts. And there is Brown Wilson, too, a link between past and present. This chapter chronicles their lives and contributions.

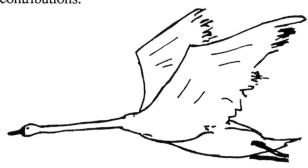

Whistling Swan

Alfred L. Kroeber

Alfred L. Kroeber (1876-1960) was probably one of the three or four most influential figures in the development of American anthropology, and made a lasting impact on the growth of knowledge about the California Indian. Although he spent the last 60 years of his life as a Californian, he actually was born on the East Coast, and grew up in New York City. His family was bilingual German and English, and the language spoken at home was German. As a child, he was also exposed to Latin and Greek, and these combined experiences instilled in him a wide ranging interest in languages. His first graduate degree at Columbia University was in fact a master's degree not in anthropology, which was at that time only a fledgling and fragmented discipline, but in English literature. With the arrival of Franz Boas on the Columbia faculty, however, Kroeber soon became fascinated with anthropology, a subject where he could follow his combined interest in natural history, linguistics, and the broader humanist perspective. His 1901 degree was one of the first Ph.D.'s in Anthropology in America.

It was the mother of William Randolph Hearst, Phoebe Hearst, whose interest in anthropology first brought Kroeber to California. Beginning in 1901, she paid his salary for his first five years as an instructor at the University of California at Berkeley. Here he began his investigations of the poorly known languages and cultures of California Indians. Throughout his forty or more years of field work and cultural/historical analysis, Kroeber attempted to reconstruct the historical linkages between adjacent and distant tribes. As with the Yokuts tribe, one of the first San Joaquin Valley tribes he visited, his purpose was "to form an estimate of an ancient, vanished culture through the medium of its modern and modified representatives."

When Kroeber died in 1960, he had been recognized by countless honors that came his way--two gold medals, five honorary degrees, and honorary membership in 16 scientific societies.

He had been the developer and head of both a great research museum and department of anthropology. And no discussion of scholarship in the world of historical anthropology can be without his name.

Alfred L. Kroeber

John Peabody Harrington

John Peabody Harrington was born at Waltham, Massachusets in a family of modest means in 1884. His family moved to Santa Barbara during his formative years. After his graduation from High School, Harrington stayed out of school for two years, and then went to Stanford where he graduated in 1905. While taking summer school courses in 1903 at the University of California, Harrington became acquainted with Kroeber, Merriam, Gifford, and other anthropologists and learned of Kroeber's trips to the San Joaquin Valley to study the Yokuts Indians.

After graduation from Stanford, Harrington went to Germany, where he studied linguistics and anthropology for two years at the Universities of Leipzig and Berlin. He came back to California and he taught modern languages at Santa Ana High School from 1906 to 1909. There he met and later married Carobeth Tucker who was a gifted student. He spent all his spare time working with Chumash, Yuman, and Mojave Indians.

He taught in universities and worked at the Archaeological Institute in Santa Fe. But, having discovered Kip-sé-paw-it, an old Chumash Indian in Santa Barbara who had a marvelous memory, he then devoted most of his time between 1912 and 1914 making a thorough study of the Chumash Indians. In 1915, he was appointed as an ethnographer with the Bureau of American Ethnology at the Smithsonian Institution in Washington D.C., a job he held for the next 39 years. He retired in 1954.

He came to the Tachi-Yokuts and other Yokuts tribes in 1914 for about two weeks to make a survey. He came again later from 1916-1920 to make a serious study of the Yokuts. At that time, he rediscovered Old Tom Atwell (who had been Kroeber's informer) and other Indians who knew about the old times and who could speak the language.

What he knew and what he taught in the universities was the science of language, or linguistics. He had a very acute ear and

24

Photo Dept. The Smithsonian

John Peabody Harrington

could discern slight differences in the sounds of speech. That ability, combined with very high intelligence and a drive to work hard without wasting any time, made him the dedicated man that he was, almost to the point of fanaticism. Linguistics was not a profession to Harrington, it was his life's work.

Harrington had developed his own way of taking notes so that he could keep up with a person talking. For instance, he did not lift his pencil from the paper in order to cross the "t" but crossed it in an individualized way the moment he wrote it. We may marvel at the man's ability to quickly put the story down on paper as it was being told.

However, he collected over and above the language itself. He let his informants ramble on and talk about things in general, as he did with Old Tom. In this way, he gained insight into the notions, fears, and superstitions that influenced his Indian informants.

He had fears, himself. He lived in terror of losing his job with the BIA (Bureau of Indian Affairs) or of being forced to go to Washington, D.C., and to remain there. This led him to be extremely secretive and to trust no one, not even his closest associates.

He retired in California and lived with friends in Santa Barbara who were closely connected with his work. When he became ill with Parkinson's disease, he remained with them until he had to go to the hospital. His daughter, Awona, heard from the BIA that her father was near death, and she found a nurse for him. He died a month later at the age of 77 in 1961.

He was an indefatigable collector of data about Indians. After his death, over 400 large boxes of notes and recordings pertaining to dozens of Indian cultures remained as a testimony to his dedication and success in his chosen career. He had a passion for privacy. In fact, he was so secretive that he would write misleading information or use abbreviations that only he could decipher, apparently fearful that someone would use his material and take credit for it. He often would not disclose the location where he was collecting information.

He seemed to be unable to organize and systematically deal with his materials. He found it more interesting to collect such data than to organize it and write reports about it. However, we are greatly indebted to this dedicated man for saving for us first-hand information of early American cultures.

At his death, the boxes of notes and recordings were sent to the Smithsonian Institution as he had directed. They had been nailed shut, addressed, and stored in church basements or with trusted individuals in the locations where he had worked.

He had come in 1916 to the Santa Rosa Rancheria and interviewed Old Bob, Yoimut (whom he knew as Josepha Damien), Luisa Brunell (who was Nick, the chief's wife), Old Tom Atwell, and others. He seemed to be interested mainly in the words of the songs (he could soon speak the Tachi language). He did not know how to write music but the Smithsonian had on its staff Helen Roberts who, with sensitive equipment, could slow down the recording and increase the volume until the words, although of low pitch, could be made out. Those old cylinders were full of scratches and squeaks and cracks that made one note repeat over and over. They were noisy and they had lost almost all of their charm, but Miss Roberts was able to produce several pages of transcriptions.[1]

Harrington made friends with all the Tachis. He visited with them each day and helped them with their chores. He learned their language, which was not difficult for this brilliant man who had studied the art of linguistics and knew how to go about it to learn a language. He wrote a vocabulary and the rules of the language.

He recorded the songs of Bob Bautista, and when that medicine man gave his annual dance on or near March first, Harrington took photos of him clad in his dance clothes, and afterwards in his regular street clothes. He had Bob construct a tule boat and took a picture of him paddling it on a pond near Burris Park.

---

[1] By "transcriptions" we mean the transfer of songs heard, onto music paper with notes.

What songs Harrington collected from the Tachis in 1916 would antedate those Cummins and others had collected. In fact, Harrington's collection was the first one after Kroeber's in 1903. But the material had not become available at all until around 1980, and then only at the Smithsonian in Washington, D.C.

When all of the boxes and other materials were received at the Smithsonian Elaine L. Mills was put in charge of the entire project.

The materials were sorted by tribes and catalogued. They included songs that were transferred from old cylinders to cassette tapes. Other items included Harrington's field notes taken when the songs were recorded, a roster of plants, animals and fish, and a vocabulary of tribal languages.

This whole procedure was multiplied by 32, which is the number of tribes he investigated. One gets an idea of the scope of the work of this brilliant man, John Peabody Harrington.

The entire collection was submitted to a publisher; all of the California chapters were sold to a consortium of California libraries and a place found to house them, the California State University at Redlands. All of that was not achieved until 1985.

Interestingly, the Folk Life Center Federal Cylinder Project has launched a project to return the copies of cylinder recordings on cassette tapes to the communities in which they were made—funded by the Ford Foundation.

Frank F. Latta

Frank Latta, in the book *California Indian Folk Lore*, gives us 32 myths which were told to him by his Indian friends. The Indian names of animals, villages, tribes, and myth-tellers are given in italics with each story. Such a style gives the whole book a sense of authenticity; it puts the reader close to the Indian and his language. A key to pronunciation is given at the beginning.[1] Also,

each story is accompanied by a picture of the animal prominent in the story, or the storyteller or by a picture of the land where the action took place. The tales are delightful and well edited by Latta, himself. While the use of italics for all of the Indian words slows the reading of the story, one feels an intimacy and a genuineness of these myths that could not be achieved in any other way.

Frank F. Latta, 1977

Latta had close associations with the old Indian storytellers who were masters of the story-telling art. He wrote:

> The entire theme was enacted as it was told. Only after close study can the trained elocutionist expect to put into the stories the little niceties of expression and inflection, along with the imitation of the various bird and animal sounds and actions that accompanied them in the old days as they were told around California campfires by the dusky-visaged Indians.

Latta was a high school history teacher in Kern and Tulare counties and spent most of his life researching and writing about San Joaquin Valley Indians and history.

---

[1] Frank F. Latta, *California Indian Folk Lore,* Shafter, CA, 1936. (Out of print).

Anna B. Gayton and the Chuckchansi-Yokuts

We have named three important sources of writings about Yokuts culture, people instrumental in preserving "Coyote" and other myths. A fourth scholar and writer was Anna Gayton. Her studies of the Chuckchansi-Yokuts living on the Fresno River near Coarsegold give us a collection of their myths and insight into the socio-political machinations made possible by chief and shaman. She published no books, and she confined her writings to reports in anthropological journals and yearbooks.

The Chuckchansi-Yokuts progressed in a different direction than the Tachi-Yokuts. Because all but two or three families had moved away or were deceased, the few who remained had been given title to land for their residences and their status as a tribe was dissolved. But, as members of the group multiplied or returned to the area, they asked the government to reinstate them as a tribe. This was accomplished.

The Chuckchansi Roundhouse

The tribe then petitioned the state for the Round House, a structure near the village of Ahwahnee. The Round House had long been used by the Miwok and Chuckchansies as a place for their tribal meetings, ceremonies and gatherings. The property was later owned by whites who used the structure as a barn for their cattle. It was in a run-down condition. The state purchased the property and then granted it to the Indians. The Chuckchansies have rebuilt the Round House with the help of some local people and it stands now as a useful monument to times of long ago.

Anna Gayton visited the Chuckchansies about 1925 and wrote of them in many articles published in journals of archaeology and ethnology.

The author of this book became acquainted with Maryan Ramirez in 1983, the guiding light for the little group of Chuckchancies. I had the pleasure of taking her a copy of Gayton and Newman's *"Yokuts and Western Mono Myths."* The mother and father and Maryan, as a young girl, were in that report, Anna Gayton having visited their home. Maryan said that she remembered one of those myths, but she never knew how it ended. It was about a basket that rolled down the hill. It was rewarding to see her satisfaction when she finally read how that myth ended. Maryan was a beautiful little lady.

Maryan Ramirez

31

Brown Wilson

Another preserver of myths is a present-day Tachi Indian, Brown Wilson of Hanford, said to be 97 years old (in 1992).

His role has not been a scholarly one like that of the other preservers just covered. However, preserver he is in the sense of having passed on Yokuts stories to other Indians and most recently of having appeared in the "How Coyote Stole the Sun" video. His father was Motsa, a big man who worked for farmers. He was a Tachi, but not a chief. Motsa and his sister had walked east from San Luis Obispo to the Indian village of Wai-u, close to the north shore of Tulare Lake. His sister died there. The sister of Tachi Tom lived at Wai-u too, and in due time she became Motsa's wife. They had a son born in a tule hut at Wai-u in about 1894. They named him Wa-sa'-pel. Thus, he was the nephew of Tachi Tom who would tell the Coyote myth to J.P. Harrington in 1916.

Motsa worked for a tobacco farmer named Antonio Wilson north of Hanford, and so he called his son Wilson, as was the custom. Later, he worked for another farmer in the same vicinity named Brown, and then they called the boy Brown Wilson.

He went to school through the second grade. He did well in arithmetic, but it was his second wife, Carrie, who taught him to read.

His first wife was Francesca. She was his cousin, his mother's brother's daughter. The Indians held strict rules against marriages between relatives as close as cousins, but the Tachi Council permitted this marriage probably because of her physical condition and maybe her financial need. Francesca was 20 years older than Brown. She had attended the Sherman Indian School near Riverside and had worked as a housemaid in Los Angeles. After an illness and operation she returned to the Tachi Rancheria where she later married Brown. They had no children. Her face was disfigured from a burn received when she was a baby, and she always wore a hat and tried to hold one hand to her face to cover the scar. Brown, in later years, always spoke kindly of Francesca.

Rantz

Brown Wilson

He was a genuine cowboy in his time and worked for ranchers around Lemoore, Armona and Hanford taking care of animals, breaking horses, shearing sheep and branding cattle. Then he worked for a man who owned a junkyard and eventually took over the business.

A person needing a spare part for an old piece of machinery to use on his farm would tryBrown's junkyard.

33

When the time came to quit and retire, he moved the old wagons, the many wagon wheels, the old farm machinery and used sinks and bathtubs that had seen better days to a residence owned by Carrie, a Portuguese woman who became his second wife. The house stood on two lots in south Hanford. The small materials — old dishes, bottles and knick-knacks — were compacted into bales with baling wire and it went there too. The bales were stacked under the grape arbor near the walnut tree and out in the open.

Brown took a group of Tachi men out west to the plains area to shear sheep one time (Frank Baga told the author about it). Every night they would gather around the fire and Brown would tell myths and stories and they would sing Tachi songs. Frank cherished his memories of this as both he and his brother, Bernard, had been sent away to Indian school when they were very young and had missed the culture training of songs and stories experienced by those who had remained at Wai-u.

He professed that he could not remember the episode in later years, perhaps fearing that this author would expect him to demonstrate.

Brown remembered his uncle coming to him for comfort when the young fellows at the rancheria would not listen to the myths. Brown was young then too, but he revered the traditions of the tribe. The culture was a part of Brown and he did not feel any need to apologize for it. Perhaps his marriage to Francesca, an older woman, had given him a more mature attitude toward the traditions.

He felt he must accept and forgive their lack of respect for tradition but remain firm in his own beliefs. And that is what he probably told Old Tom, his uncle.

In 1986, Brown coached Susan Devany in the Tachi dialect of the Yokuts language when she studied at the University of California in the linguistics department.

CHAPTER IV

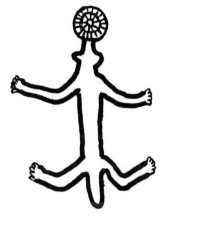

THE YOKUTS CULTURE

Introduction to the Yokuts Culture

The Yokuts had a distinctive culture developed over several thousand years. A culture in general is defined as the sum of traits held in common to define a way of life of a people. The term culture may be divided into two parts: material culture and non-material culture. Material culture is defined as the methods and materials used in the process of providing food, clothing, and shelter; non-material culture is defined as activities such as social, political and ceremonial behavior and those beliefs as implied in religion. Also in this last category come accomplishments in the fine arts, such as oral language, music, and basketry and other activities that are creative and that express the aesthetic, artistic, and emotional needs of the people. It is with the last three that we are to be mainly involved in this study of Yokuts culture: (1) the myth, an expression of the language arts; (2) the songs, representative of their music; and (3) basketry, a craft that can be elevated to an art, as the reader shall see.

The study of a culture must be related to a specific time period because cultures evolve and change. Cultural evolution is a constant process, and groups are continually borrowing from their neighbors as well as developing more or less original traits. A culture sometimes loses features—features that it took a few thousand years to evolve but which, with changes in living conditions, are no longer needed. The time period we are concerned with here is the early twentieth century (the time of Kroeber and Harrington) and the time when this author knew a little group of Tachi-Yokuts singers in 1940.

We can see some of the changes that have occurred in the evolution of the Yokuts culture as it has emerged from the early days commencing with the so-called "discovery" by the Spanish in 1772 through the time of our recorded myth in the early 1900s and the visits of Kroeber and Harrington and up to the Yokuts of the present day, 1992.

The culture of the Yokuts today of course differs from that of the time period of the early part of the twentieth century. The rude cabins of the earlier time have been replaced with housing that could be typical of middle class suburbia. Today's Yokuts shop for food the same as other people, and they are fond of hot dogs, hamburgers, and soft drinks.

Most of these Indians profess the Catholic faith and attend church in towns and cities nearest their homes; however, there is a Catholic church built in 1987 on the Tachi Rancheria south of Lemoore. Children attend public schools near their homes and in some cases graduate from high school and go on to junior college.

A federally-funded "Head Start" activity at the Rancheria

Head Start is available in some locations where, besides English, they learn a few words of the Yokuts language. Today, Indians can have most of the advantages of modern living; but they still retain some of their Yokuts culture.

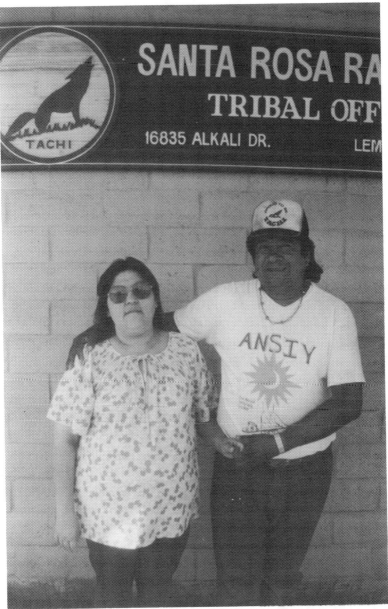

Photo by Hanford Sentinel

Santa Rosa Rancheria's Audrey and Clarence Atwell, Jr.
The couple represented the Indian Rancheria in the Hanford
Homecoming Parade in May, 1990

After 1772, when explorers, traders, priests and other visitors began to come into the valley, cholera, typhoid fever, smallpox and measles would attack and sicken whole villages of Indians. Immunity or partial immunity protected the white people whose forbears in Europe, after plagues had swept across the continent for many years, had developed antigens in their blood for defeating those diseases. But the Indians would sicken, spend a few hours in the sweat house (their only way of treating such diseases) and they would succumb. Syphilis was another enemy which attacked the Indians. These were enemies from within, and it is difficult to comprehend their total effect on the decline of Indian culture.

A recent author writes, "From the time of the first white contacts, observers judged the Indians of California to be exceedingly primitive and viewed their cultures with boundless disdain and contempt."[1] White people called the California Indians "diggers" and thought of them as being of no value.

According to the changing needs of white observers, Indians were seen first as victims, then as a cheap labor force, and so, useful. Later, at the time of the gold rush, they were seen simply as obstacles to be eliminated and still later, as vaqueros, farm workers and servants. The incoming Americans in California saw the treatment of Indians as reflecting the denigration begun by the traditions of the Spanish empire-- "enslavement" and mistreatment. The Americans could have rescued the Indians from such poor treatment, but they did not.

Even Jededia Smith, a trapper who was strongly religious, wrote that the assessment of the culture of California Indians by many old settlers was that the Indians were very primitive and worthless. He, himself, had a poor opinion of them.

Recent increased interest in anthropology and archaeology among all people has opened new vistas to those who share the

---

[1]James J. Rawls, *Indians of California: The Changing Image*, Norman: University of Oklahoma Press, 1984.

valley with these early travelers. Attention and study has rewarded all with an increased understanding of this culture. The relations between whites and Indians have been poor at times and Indians have been deeply wounded. Whites, too, have been hurt and frustrated when, with the best of intentions, their motives have been misunderstood.

Why is it that among themselves, here in the valley only one Indian war has taken place in the remembrance of the Indians while, in the world arena, whites have had one war after another? In the history chapter in this book the reader will find the story of that one war, the Tule River Indian War of 1856.

* * * * * * * * *

In the meanwhile, it is time to take another look at Yokuts culture.

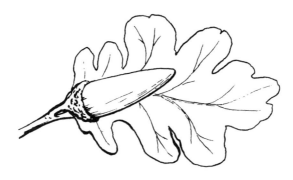

The following section will focus on specific aspects of the Yokuts culture: their myths, their songs, their basketry, and other areas such as the rock paintings, dancing and religion.

A Trader Visits the Tribe Before 1772

Very few of the valley Indians ventured beyond the boundaries agreed upon as the territory of the tribe. But there were traders among the Indians whose business was walking over well-defined trails carrying products from one tribe to the next — and beyond.

We can picture one coming to a Yokuts village in the valley after traveling from somewhere east of the Sierras. The Win.á-tun who lived at the edge of the Yokuts village would greet him and take him to the chief of the tribe where he would unwrap and display articles for trade acquired from other Indians on his journey. Perhaps there were pinon nuts or obsidian from the Monos who lived on the east side of the Sierra. Certainly there would be roots of the bracken fern used in making the dark design on baskets. These would be exchanged for dried fish and tule roots from the lake, or goose and duck eggs, or deer, elk and antelope skins, or baskets.

At such a meeting would be the chief and his family, the extended family, and the shaman. These would listen to all the traveler had to tell as the barter and trading went on. Perhaps the visitor would talk of coming through a pass in the snow, of the huge rock (Moro Rock) high on the mountain, and about the great trees that grew there. It would give rise to much wonder and awe as he told about these stupendous features of nature.

The shaman or medicine man would think of them as proof of the mighty power underlying all experience, and these would be the forces to which he would appeal when asking for supernatural power.

In listening to the talk of the elders, the family of the chief would be acquiring an education at this meeting with the one who had traveled so far. They would discuss these things among themselves at a later time and recall every word that was said.

In this way, the chief, the shaman, and the family of the chief became much more knowledgeable than the rest of the tribe. So when the chief was dying, or even before, he would select a son, usually the eldest son, to succeed him as chief. Or it could be his brother, or his grandson that he selected, and, when voted by the tribe, that one would become chief.

Myths, a Part of Culture

The myths were a part of the Yokuts culture based on the environment in which the Indians lived—its trees, rivers, streams, lakes, swamps, and sloughs. The animals were part of that environment too—the grizzly bear, the coyote, the squirrels, and rabbits, and the birds. They are all there, eulogized and sung about. And the animals talked like men. The culture of the Indians was intimately related to the natural world about them. Yokuts Indian myths, as collected by Kroeber, Harrington, Gayton, Newman and Latta are based on the very nature of this valley, the San Joaquin.

The plots of myths were often borrowed from or loaned to other Yokuts tribelets--there were no sharply defined boundaries. "The Theft of the Sun" myth was a major myth of Central Valley Yokuts. It was known by all the Yokuts tribelets around the Tulare Lake basin and those to the north of that lake; known even to some tribes of the Sacramento Valley and surprisingly to some in the state of Washington.

The people who ventured into the New World from across the Bering Strait, 12,000 or more years ago, brought their culture with them. There was language, of course. They had already developed language in order to communicate with one another for their success in hunting, mostly the larger animals. But they would probably have had little leisure time to develop the arts, except for stories, myths and tales told around the campfires at night--and songs. The latter were probably of a primitive type, not like the songs given here as sung by Old Bob and Salt Lake Pete at the beginning of the twentieth century.

It is interesting that these wandering people had myths. Several years ago, A.F. Kroeber and E. W. Gifford[1] each collected myths from the Karok tribe in the northwestern interior of California.

One myth depicts the story of an old man who put up long poles into a tree. It seems that the old man had designs on the young man's wife and this was his strategy to rid himself of the competition. When the young man had climbed to the greatest height, the old man then removed the poles altogether, leaving the youth stranded.

That same plot was found in a myth of the Bororo Indians of central Brazil by an ethnologist, Levi-Strauss. The Karok tribe of northwestern California may have been neighbors of the Brazilian tribe, either in their homeland or at times when they settled down along the way.

Myths are a study in themselves. The tale-types or plots, have been analyzed and numbered. When the same type is found in tribal lore in tribes widely separated geographically, it gives rise to speculation that they migrated from the same area, that they shared a culture, a language, and stories. After they crossed Bering Strait, it is thought that some went on to the south and the east, still others stopped in their wanderings or perhaps took a detour to California.

The flora and fauna of the arctic regions were left behind as the Indians traveled southward. New animals and trees appeared on the horizon beckoning them to follow. New fruits and seeds developed from the glorious blooms of spring. The myths, stories and songs changed too, to reflect the new environment. Coyote has many adventures as trickster and hero, and the stories about him explain the features of the new land where they found themselves.

Kroeber lamented,[2] "If only we really knew them," and further wrote, "It would be strange if the Yokuts, a large and prosperous block of people, had not developed a culture which should display

---

[1] *Karok Myths*, {Compiled by} A.L. Kroeber and E.W. Gifford; edited by Grace Buzaljko, Berkeley: University of California Press, 1980.

[2] A.L. Kroeber, *Handbook of the Indians of California*, Berkeley: California Book Co., 1953, p. 543.

many novelties, a quantity of interesting peculiarities." So, in 1903 when Kroeber was in the valley studying the Yokuts, he seemed to sense that the uncommunicated meanings of the myths, implicit in the setting and inherent in the language, had not been disclosed to him. In other words, Kroeber suspected that there were hidden meanings in the myths. The opinion of this author is that secret meanings in the myths were hidden in the language itself.[1] That dual feature of language which altered the meanings of a word by adding suffixes, paired with an altered form of the verb accompanying it, gave aesthetic satisfaction. As long as the Yokuts continued to speak their own language, this would hold true. But, their language was gradually being replaced, first by Spanish, and then by English, and now, in 1992, only a few elders can speak their own language. The myths were on the way to obscurity even as Harrington was collecting them.

Kroeber's skeletonized translations[2] show only the plots of many of the myths he collected. The niceties of agreement of added suffixes of the noun with the altered verb are entirely lost in translation because English has no parallel of such a linguistic feature.

Kroeber wrote, "The real merits of their folklores lies implicit in a background or setting of which the skeletonized translations give to us but rudimentary hints."[3] Now, that background or setting has been changed drastically; the swamps drained, canals dug, and dams built in the mountains on all the rivers and sizeable streams and lately laser-leveling that eradicates every small hillock and fills in every depression, so that we see a truly industrialized agriculture.

---

[1] See the discussion of Characteristic and Stylistic Features of the Yokuts Language in this book.

[2] See the myth from Kroeber's notes in the examples section of the chapter on myths in this book. It shows what is meant by skeletonized translations.

[3] A.L. Kroeber, *Handbook of the Indians of California*, Bureau of American Ethnology, Bulletin 78: Smithsonian Institution, 1925, p. 541.

There is hardly a vestige of the original landscape that once made up the background of the valley.

The wild animals that once freely roamed the valley are gone — or almost gone. Once in a while, a coyote will come out of the foothills and give a moonlight serenade to the few farms reaching out from the plains. The grizzly bear had to go; he was a dangerous animal; the snakes and mosquitos are not missed either.

Joseph Campbell and Myths of the World

Joseph Campbell made a comprehensive study of cultures, especially myths, of peoples and tribes all over the world.[1] One tribe he studied did not even know how to make a fire until a visitor recently showed them the way.[2] Another tribe lived in caves and wore no clothes.[3] Some tribes were Stone Age primitives, others had a more complex culture. In the main: all had some religion, all solemnized marriages, and all buried their dead. Campbell believed that uniform ideas obtained by peoples unknown to each other must have a common ground of truth. "There must be," Campbell says, "a common ground in the psyche." The idea, expressed differently by C.G. Jung, was "archetypes of the collective unconscious." To put it another way, the subconscious mind in each of us can see signs and symbols that are in common to all of us.

---

[1] Joseph Campbell, "Historical Atlas of World Mythology," Vol. I, Part I. pp. 103-125 New York: Vander Marck Editions, 1988..

[2] The Adamanese, who live on islands south of Burma.

[3] The Tasaday of Mindanao of the southern Philipine Islands.

Campbell was awed and greatly impressed by the Paleolithic master artists who painted landscapes and animals in the caves of southern France. "They were created with the eye of the mind, not the eyes of the physical look of things," he said. "They give us a pictorial script, a truly amazing testament of Stone Age times," he wrote.[1] With the paintings as a backdrop, undoubtedly many rites were practiced, but they have not been saved for us because early man had no written language. The paintings are credited to Neanderthal man who made these paintings about 20,000 B.C.(or earlier).

Campbell's Opinions

"The human race has evolved in the way of a single unfolding life through its millions of apparently separate individuals, in all quarters of the earth and through all weatherings.[2] Homo Sapiens sapiens (modern man), was attained in all quarters simultaneously while earth was going through world-shaking changes."

"As to the myths: there are so many having parallel plots among peoples having no connection with each other; and as to the ceremonies, there are so many similar ceremonies among various peoples of separate climates, - (and there he speaks again of the ceremonies of religion, marriage, and the burial of the dead) that we seemingly must assume the existence of a collective psychic substratum."[2]

We also must regard myths, songs, and ceremonies as revealed in dreams and trance as outward expressions of this collective unconscious. When I say we, I mean this author and, possibly, the reader of this book.

---

[1] Joseph Campbell, *The Power of the Myth*, New York: Doubleday, 1988, p71.

[2] Ibid.

Simply put, a myth is a traditional or legendary story, usually concerning some superhuman being.

What did Joseph Campbell have to say about myths of California tribes, especially Yokuts myths? He writes about the character Coyote, the trickster. "The traits of the trickster," says Campbell, "has had appeal for mankind from the very beginnings of civilization." In the myth "How Coyote Stole the Sun," we see the trickster in the response of Coyote when asked where he came from and if there were people down there. Coyote replied, "Come from South, there are lots of people down there." But, says the storyteller, in truth there were only two, Eagle and Coyote. "The reaction of the audience in aboriginal societies to both Coyote and his exploits is prevailingly one of laughter, tempered by awe,"[1] wrote Campbell.

Campbell goes on to say, "Many of the trickster traits were perpetuated in the figure of the medieval jester (in European cultures), and have survived right up to the present day in the Punch and Judy plays and in the clown."[2]

Although Campbell outlines culture areas of North America, his treatment of area no. 6 is brief and disappointing. He classifies "the Far West, the Great Basin, and California as the early hearth of the Desert Culture, where it persisted into historic times," and provides only the tantalizing comment, "Tribes of the area were the master basket weavers of the continent."[2]

---

[1] Joseph Campbell, *Historical Atlas of World Mythology*, Vol. I, Part 2, "Mythologies of the Great Hunt," New York: Vander Marck Editions, 1988, pp. 196 and 201.

[2] Gleanings from the book *Primitive Mythology* by Joseph Campbell, writing about his reading and his experiences in the far north of Siberia.

Of course, Campbell's subject area was so vast that we cannot expect him to have explored, studied, and formed an opinion of the particular tribe that we happen to be interested in here. His is a magnificent work, however, possibly with too wide a scope to be attempted by one man in his lifetime. When he died at the age of 83, in 1987, he left an astounding array of works; the volume cited on the previous page is in fact part of a set of books still being published for the first time in the years after his death.

Shamans submitted to fasting at frequent intervals. Fasting was considered the best means of attaining knowledge of hidden things. They often kept the strictest diet and they even fasted before an event if they would have to call upon their powers. The following paragraph gives the sort of beliefs and activities of a shaman.

> He could reach behind the veil and touch those hidden centers that break the normal natural circuits of energy and create transformations. He could cause ectoplasmic emanations. He could take the form of a beast, conjure up or dispel a storm, and tell myths as though reciting tales of his own intimate knowledge and experience, the mythological lore and legends of the tribe.

So we see that Old Bob, the medicine man of the Tachi-Yokuts was not out of line in trying to tell the myth of the theft of the sun (see page 55). He was handicapped by the two languages, thinking in one language and speaking in the other, and probably also by lack of practice in telling the story.

Language and Myths

This little analysis of Yokuts language is based on a report by Anna Gayton and Stanley S. Newman, both of whom collected Yokuts myths around the 1930s. They collaborated in writing a report entitled *Yokuts and Western Mono Myths* in which several of the Yokuts myths are translated into English. Each of them wrote about some of the features of the Yokuts language which revealed the unique and original charm of that language. Newman's writing of *Linguistic Aspects of Yokuts' Style*, a sub-title of the introductory Part I of the report, is explored briefly here. Some of the intricate details of grammar are left out as it is this author's purpose merely to tell in general what Newman observed about the Yokuts language.

Students can see examples of the Yokuts language and how it is put together by studying Yokuts myths. First of all, they need to keep in mind that "Yokuts is not a peculiar and imperfect kind of English."[1]

Secondly, the ideas expressed in their myths are of a very general nature. They are bare and simple and without a complicated structure. The reader is directed to see the myth taken from Kroeber's notes on page 53 in this book. Thirdly, they added suffixes to words but not more than three suffixes to any one word.

By adding suffixes to a word, the meaning of that word could be changed, enlarged, or modified, and that is practically the only way that a word meaning could be enhanced. But, adding a suffix also affects the verb form. Thus, "a grammatical system operates" and it "reveals a formal balance and symmetry that is rare among languages." Acknowledging that this system creates little in enhancing meanings, Newman wrote, "it adds a great deal to the esthetic pleasure of both listener and speaker."[1] Newman wrote of the impossibility of capturing these aspects of a language in an English translation.

---

[1] The Yokuts language has its own rules and those rules are, and must be, strictly followed.

51

He concluded his portion of the chapter with the following summary: *"Yokuts is a type of collective expression that values balance of inner form, and restraint in the representation of meanings."* And then, recalling the spurious and frustrating feeling in reading a translation of a bare, skeletonized Yokuts myth, (and for a sample, read the one recorded by Kroeber in the following pages), he says again, *"Yokuts is not a peculiar and imperfect kind of English."*[1]

In other words, Newman saw the Yokuts language as exemplified in the myth, as a unique, rather quaint expression of oral language that valued the inner balance and symmetry of its construction, rather than the details of meanings. The literary goals of the two languages are not the same. We should never judge one culture by the standards of another culture; but we should instead remind ourselves of the different goals of the two. In this author's estimation the Yokuts language had some of the qualities of a work of art.

After all, the "grammatical system" noted by Newman in the above may have a parallel in English. The feature of the English language that would come nearest to such a device would possibly be <u>rhyming</u>. We ourselves adore rhymes, and will endure almost any simple plot for its sake. An example would be the Dr. Seuss book *The Cat in the Hat*, a book for young children. However, the Yokuts never seemed to have hit upon rhyme as a way of matching endings of words.

---

[1] Arna H. Gayton and Stanley S. Newman, *Yokuts and Western Mono Myths*, Berkeley, Los Angeles, University of California Press, 1940, p. 4-8.

Examples of Myths

A portion of a Yokuts Myth from A.L. Kroeber's Notes of 1903

At put everywhere water.
A tell flew up out of water to sky.
Had nest in tree.
They stayed there never saw earth, only water.
Youlitc (wolf), Kaiyi (Coyote), wehisit (Panther);
Troxil (Eagle) (Eagle was the captain),
Limic (Prairie Hawk),
Poyon (hawk - a swift one), Wit-(condor).[1]
Eagle thinking about making earth.
"Will have to make earth." called Kui Kui
(small duck in water, never fly).

"Go down get earth," He never got. Died.
Called a duck. "Come here," wanted him to go down.
When went, way down, got mud.
When touched with hands, died. When died, came up.
Eagle and nest of swan saw dirt in fingernail.
Eagle, when saw took dirt,
took telie and pele (2 kinds grass seeds)
mixed with ground dirt,
made mush or dough with water mixed.

In morning put in water,
It swelled all overspread, went mountainward,
(the seeds when mixed with water swell).
Eagle, "Take dirt."
Then those in tree went and took Night.
Eagle said this,

---

[1] Indiscriminate use of capital letters in these four lines are as given in Kroeber's notes.

"Early morn when morning star come, tila wolf, Holler."
Then wolf hollered, and earth went away again,
but they had dirt in nest; and all was water again.
Eagle said, "We make again."
Took two kinds seeds put with water, swelled out again.
Night. Morning Star came..
Eagle said to wolf, "Talk again."
Hollered again three times, and earth was tremblor,
but was o.k...
Coyote said then, "I have to holler too."
Hollered and earth shook a little.
Now was good. . . , (continued).

Old Bob[1] Tells a Myth

The following episode is drawn from Harrington's notes taken in 1916.

Harrington got his camera, tripod, film, and paper. The oranges and apples he brought soon disappeared. They (the Indians) sat down on benches waiting for the dance.

<u>Harrington wrote:</u>

Robert began to tell the story, and he got the English language mixed up with the Tachi language. It was supposed to be about Coyote and Eagle, who was Coyote's uncle. Eagle's house was inside the solid boulder. I could not understand the story because of the twisted English. It lasted at least 15 minutes. Bob mentioned a big fire where the sun was. Coyote thought he would go up there and look at the sun. He wanted to get to the sun. He wanted to get to the sun to see whether it was fastened up or not. Coyote, when he looked at the sun, made himself into a stick of green wood. They threw Coyote on the big fire near the sun, but he was a stick of green wood, green wood that wouldn't burn. Thus he got a good look at the sun. They threw him out of the fire because he wouldn't burn.

The next thing was that he grabbed the sun and started off with it, but as he stole the sun, he scattered the big fire and it burned the buzzard's head and made it bald. It burned black marks under and around the eyes of a certain kind of fowl. It burned many animals. Animals have burned marks on them. They all ran after Coyote. He was so tripne {magic} they would nearly get him, and then he would run off.

The next thing was that he took the sun back to Eagle's house. Then his uncle told him that he was afraid that the sun would burn them all up, there at the lake. The uncle told him to take it way off. Coyote took it way off where the sun rises.

---

[1] More about Robert Bautista, "Old Bob," on page 69.

Before he put it off farther there was a conversation between Coyote and his uncle, "Did they catch you?" said Eagle. "No, they didn't catch me," said Coyote.

Bob always made Coyote talk in a soprano voice. ("Did not get the rest clearly," wrote Harrington.)

Giants

Harrington asked Tom if he knew anything about the large bones found sometimes when whites dug a very deep hole.

Tom said, "The first people were big fellows (gesture to show gigantic stature). When they died anyplace, they took them down to Heinlen's place. Put their bodies there. Every evening at six o'clock the bones come out, and in the morning they go back in again. Where they come out is where the hillock is there. When Tom was camping there, when he made the fence, he used to see them coming out every night, and morning there would be nothing there. Maybe not so now.

Informer also knows of the bones that were found near Jacobs School. Just the same. The first people would run and jump and fall down. Their bones would break. People had measing (measles?) and said it was no good.

Tom was right: those were big fellows. They undoubtedly were large mammals such as roamed in the valley up to 10,000 years ago, and then gradually became extinct. In the light of later knowledge all of us are better informed. Those animals probably were the mammoth and the mastodon.

Jacobs School was made over from a residence and was situated at the edge of the lake. It is possible that to use it for a school, a deeper well was needed. Bones of those large animals were to be found deep in the soil which had been washed down from the surrounding mountains for thousands and thousands of years.[1]

---

[1] Many valley museums display fossilized bones of these giant creatures. They are seen at the Kings County Museum in Burris Park, the Fresno Metropolitan Museum, the Baker Museum in Coalinga, and others. Most were discovered as workmen dug canals, drilled for oil or excavated for roadways.

Tom used the topic of conversation to introduce another little folk tale. He said:

* * * * * * * * *

"There was a tiny kind of lizard. He sat up there at night and made talk, and said, 'Make people like me,' he said to those giants. They heard him but they said they wanted people a little bigger, but otherwise would have them just like him. Roadrunner said he wanted people to have three fingers (he has 3) and the little lizard did not like three fingers."

"No, it won't hold," said Little Lizard, and he handed Roadrunner a stick to test him. Roadrunner gripped the stick as hard as he could but as he twisted and turned his foot, he lost hold and the stick fell from his grasp.

Lizard grasped the stick then, and as he grasped the stick, turned and twisted every way, he held it tightly. That is why people have five fingers and toes on their arms and legs, but birds, like the roadrunner, have only three.[1]

---

[1] J.P. Harrington, "The Papers of J.P. Harrington." available at the California State University Library at Riverside, California.

Miss Slight Says

Tom wished desperately to interest the young fellows at the rancheria in the myths he knew, but he only provoked their ridicule. The school teacher at the rancheria told Harrington what happened[1].

"Some of the young fellows went over to Tom's place," she said, "and started cutting on a little tree there. Tom objected and told them to stop. These were the fellows who did not want to listen to Tom telling the myths. One fellow told Tom, 'This is my place, I can chop this tree down if I want' (the Indians thought all of the land belonged to them; white people like Atwell had no right to it). Tom remonstrated, but he was no match for the husky youths. He came for comfort to his nephew, Brown Wilson, then barely 20 years old."

"He cried and cried," said Brown . "He want show how they u'do and all 'at ki' of 'tuff" (how they used to do and all that kind of stuff) and Brown indicated with his hands the motions that might be used in telling a myth. "How they do," he said, "but he—not," and Brown shook his head. "He didn' have quite enough power. Now,— no more!"[2]

---

[1] From the notes of J. P. Harrington.

[2] Interview with Brown Wilson in 1987.

Miss Slight (the schoolteacher) asked Bob if he ever made up songs. Bob answered saying, "The songs coming up out of the lake, or the wind over the lake, is like women singing. That is the way I found them." "He always uses the verb, to find {found} for to remember, {remember},"[1] said Miss Slight.

* * * * * * * * * * *

The songs coming up out of the lake,
Or the wind over the lake
Is like women singing.
That is the way I remember them.

Robert, Tachi Medicine Man

After I was dancing all night,
I called out to the Morning Star.
It helped me—
And they all came and helped me

Robert (paraphrased)

---

[1] From Harrington's notes, in "Papers of John P. Harrington" in the Library of CSU Riverside, Riverside, CA. (Notes were under Harrington's caption, "Miss Slight Says"), n.b. The "Papers" are being published in book form under the title "The Papers of John P. Harrington and Carobeth Laird." Carobeth accompanied him in most of his travels in the San Joaquin Valley and copied his notes in readable longhand.

SAPÁGAY

Maria Solaris' mother, Brigida, had a brother (a half brother) by the name of Sapágay, who was a famous shaman at Tinliu in the Tejon country where some Yokuts Indians lived. Maria, who was a Chumash, went by way of the Cuyama River from Santa Barbara to the Tejon area.

They said Sapágay knew both black and white magic and he could make a skeleton rise by means of some kind of mineral (alum? used as medicine or poison). "He could run after an antelope and overtake it as easily as a man could catch a little child," they said.

This is the story of Juan Moynol {a Tachi, who lived near the Tejon region} who had a great swelling on his neck. There was a little old man in the village. Sapágay and the little old man danced, and singers with split stick rattles sang. Sapágay lightly touched the sick man's neck with his feather stick. Suddenly two xelex (falcons) came and perched on the sick man's shoulders and people heard coyotes calling out right in the middle of the crowd. The little old man began to cry, and Sapágay said, "He will get well." Then the xelex flew away. The next day Juan Moynal, the sick man, was better. He was cured.

Sapágay said, "When I die, don't bury me in the ground. Leave me on top of the ground in the cemetery." Then Sapágay died and after the funeral ceremonies, three old women who were in charge, left his body at the edge of the grave that night. The next morning the body had disappeared. Sapágay appeared again three days later.

Leon Manuel's Indian name was David Sapágay. He lived in Reedley part of the time and was a good Tachi-Yokuts singer. He claimed the famous shaman was his grandfather. Further unusual happenings were recorded by Harrington when he went to the Tejon region, and Blackburn incorporated them in his book.[1]

---

[1] Thomas C. Blackburn, *December's Child*, Berkeley: Univ. of California Press, 1975, pp. 266-272.

THE PEOPLING OF CALIFORNIA

The basket weavers often used designs in their baskets that represented dreams or visions, or motifs to which they could appeal when in distress. They could represent the sun, moon, lightning, the rainbow, a butterfly, snakes, or other images that were meaningful. Seldom would they reveal the meaning and interpret the patterns to those outside of their most intimate circle--but occasionally, an exception would be made.

On the following page is a legend told by a Saboba Indian of San Jacinto in Southern California. She was the last one of her tribe and the last one to know and tell the legend. Her basket was woven with a design to remind herself and preserve for others the legend of her ancestors. As she kept her eyes on her basket, she told the history of her people.[1]

On the basket, the circles around the base represent the villages of the Sabobas, and the link that binds them together. Mountains and valleys in which the villages were located are depicted in the band above the villages. Peeping over the rim are figures representing the sun, moon, and morning star, and the like, showing that "those above" were still watching over them.

---

[1] George Wharton James, *Indian Basketry*, 3rd ed., New York: H. Malkan, pp. 217-220. 1903.

THE LEGEND
(A Shortened Version)

She told of her people leaving their dark land in boats and landing on these shores, that there occured a great earth-quake and storm. They were fearful and waited for a sign. But, none came. Only silence came.

Then a gentle light appeared in the east and it gradually filled the sky with glory. After that their god took some of the people and made them into animals, birds and fish; plants, flowers and trees; snakes, reptiles and insects.

The people were to be friends, tied together by kinship, kindness and peace.

Dancing

There was always dancing when two or more tribelets met together. All would join hands and walk in a circle, going to the right while singing a friendship song and then reverse and circle to the left as another part (stanza) of the song was sung. This gave the young men a chance to dance next to the girl of his choice and was a way of a youth meeting a prospective mate.

Besides the group dances, there were quite a few character dances such as the Coyote Dance and the Bear Dance. One character dance was of the Ho-oo-no described in detail by Yoimut for F.F. Latta.[1]

"Ho-oo-no was dressed in a long pretty blue dress that covered his head and reached to the ground with armholes cut out for the arms. The skin and feathers from the necks of the fish cranes covered the blue cloth on his head. Two large, round pieces of abalone were attached to the cloth to look like eyes and there were peep-holes cut out below so that he could see. Long, blue wing feathers from fish cranes were fastened to a skirt of strings. These feathers would swing loose as Ho-oo-no danced.

"On his back across his shoulders a stick was attached and loosely fastened to it were about ten short pieces of bamboo the size of oversized pencils. When he danced Ho-oo-no would jerk his shoulders and make the bamboo sticks rattle together."

"Ho-oo-no would dance lightly on his feet," Yoimut said, "with whirls and turns across the enclosure where members of the tribe sat in a semi-circle." He called 'Ho-oo-no', and whistled low. People hid things in the grass or in a tree in the afternoon before the dance and that night he would swoop and circle and then call out 'Ho-oo-no' and point to the spot where something was hidden. The person who had hidden the thing to which he was pointing was then obliged to come and pick it up and give it to the dancer.

---

[1] F.F. Latta, *Handbook of the Yokuts Indians*, 2nd ed. rev., Santa Cruz: Bear State Books, 1977.

Thus the people were able to entertain themselves at their gatherings; children would squeal with fear and delight as he lunged toward them and said the magic words, 'Ho-oo-no' and he, himself, would have the pleasure of portraying all the graceful motions of the fish crane which he had observed in some of the lazy afternoons among the tules at the edge of the lake.

As to the Coyote Dance, what we have is the recording of the Coyote Dancing Song by Salt Lake Pete and taken by Kroeber in 1903. That is probably the most authentic description we are ever to have. It is seen through the ears and lost to the eyes for almost a hundred years.

In the Bear Dance, the owner of a bear hide (with the fur left on) was the one most likely to be asked to perform. The person taking the part of the bear would thrust hands and feet through strips sewed on the inside of the bear's four feet, the bear's head on top of and forward of his own head. He would be led in. There would be grunts, growls and snarls. Occasionaly, he would rise on hind legs and scan the horizon as bears do. Then he would be led away by someone having hold of a rope around his neck.

Songs, a Part of Culture

Eagle, Coyote and other animals are prominent not only in Yokuts myths (as we have seen) but in their songs as well.

As the ethnologists were collecting myths, they often collected songs at the same time. Many were recorded and are available to listen to today.

The Tachi-Yokuts at the rancheria south of Lemoore have received a kit of 8 cassette tapes of their songs as recorded from 1903-1965 with a catalog of explanations. The kit also contains songs by the Tule River Yokuts, the Chukchansi-Yokuts of Coarsegold, and chants (songs to accompany legends) of the Miwok, sung by Chris Brown (Chief Leeme) of Yosemite, a Miwok (not Yokuts). A copy of the kit containing cassette tapes and catalog, has been presented to the Kings County Library by this author.

The following have made the largest collection of songs, although there were others who collected one or two:

In 1903, A.L. Kroeber, an anthropologist from the University of California visited the tribe. He collected both songs and myths. The songs are on cassette tapes at the Lowie Museum at the University of California at Berkeley.

In 1916-1920, John P. Harrington and his wife, Carobeth, were there. His collection of songs are on cassette tapes at the Smithsonian Institution in Washington, D.C.

In 1925, Helen Roberts came and recorded 94 songs from Old Bob. Her transcriptions and songs are in two notebooks in the Folk Music Department at the Library of Congress, Washington, D.C.

My own recordings were done in 1940. They are related in a book, *The Tachi-Yokuts, Their Lives, Songs and Stories*, published in 1978-79, available from the author at 2064 Carter Way, Hanford, CA 93230.

In 1949, Frank F. Latta published his book which includes some words of songs, published by Bear State Books, Santa Cruz, Ca.

In 1955, the L. Arthur Barr, Co., which made movies, also made some recordings.

In 1958, James Hatch, a student at U.C. Berkeley, came. He contributed a paper to Kroeber's Anthropological Society Papers. He recorded and transcribed a Yokuts story and 12 songs. These are available at U.C. Library at Berkeley.

In 1959, Alfred Petroforte wrote a book, *Songs of the Tachis and Piutes*, Naturegraph Publishers, Happy Camp, CA., 1965.

In 1978, Dr. Louis Ballard of Santa Fe, New Mexico, recorded some songs. He was later on the Board of the National Endowment for the Humanities.

THE HISTORY OF YOKUTS SONGS

We should not think of the Yokuts songs presented here in this book as primitive. To hear truly primitive songs now one would have to look for primitive or half-civilized tribes in the far corners of the world, such as in the Islands of Micronesia. You can sometimes hear such singing in documentaries of these far-away places--songs on a single pitch, long sustained, sung by a group, perhaps a group of women, producing a tone sung with a single syllable on the one pitch. The tone is sustained by having each member of the group take a breath at a different time.

As an example, in the motion picture "Lawrence of Arabia," the women of the tribe sang such a song. In their black robes they placed themselves on each side of the narrow pass and filled the air with their singing. As their camel-mounted warriors filed through the pass and began a dangerous thrust across the vast desert, the sustained, wordless tone of the ancient song fortified their courage. It followed them until they could no longer hear it and it remained in their memories with all they held dear--their women, their children, their tribal home.

Bruno Nettl, a professor at Indiana University, has made a study of the various historical phases of tribal singing in a book titled *North American Indian Musical Styles*.[1] He reviewed quantities of transcriptions of Indian melodies that had been transcribed into music notation.

He concluded that we will never know exactly what the California Yokuts Indian songs were like in the very earliest of times. But we may infer that the present style of singing of the various tribes has evolved from the primitive over thousands of years.

---

[1] Bruno Nettl, *North American Indian Musical Styles,* Philadelphia: American Folklore Society, 1954.

THE KROEBER COLLECTION

When Kroeber visited the San Joaquin Valley in 1903, early in his studies of California Indians, he recorded the songs sung by Roberto (Bob) Bautista and Salt Lake Pete, both Yokuts.

While quite a young man, Bob Bautista had an uncle who was a medicine man for the Kaweah-Yokuts tribe, a tribe living near the foothills on the Kaweah River where Terminus Dam is now. When his uncle died, Bob elected to succeed him and was heir to his uncle's sacred objects; but as Bob was a Tachi, he continued to live with the Tachis at Tulare Lake. There he developed a large repertoire of songs and was highly regarded among the Tachis.

Old Bob with split-stick rattles   The Smithsonian

They believed he had POWER. Bob married. His marriage was not permanent, but he did have two or three children.

Bob made adobe bricks for Uncle Dan Rhoads in 1856 for what is now called the Lemoore Adobe. It has been preserved and still stands near highway 41 about two miles northwest of Lemoore. The name Bautista appears as one of the signers of the notorious 18 treaties, signing for the Kaweah-Yokuts Tribe. This man could have been Bob's uncle, the medicine man for the Kaweahs.

(Another name appearing for the Kaweahs was Francisco, the chief, who caused the frightful massacre of the John Woods Party in 1850. More of this in Chapter VI).

The Smithsonian

Roberto Bautista, "Old Bob," dancing in 1916. Carobeth Harrington, wife of John Harrington and an ethnologist herself, is seated on the ground behind the stool.

After visiting the rancheria and recording Bob's songs in 1903, Professor Kroeber took Bob and Josepha Damien down to the Ventura County Fair. Bob had been asked by the authorities at the fair to make a tule boat, and he was busily weaving in and out some tule leaves when Kroeber came up to him. (Tule boats were made of the round-stemmed tules tied together in bundles and lashed together in a boat shape. Their pithy centers assured their lightness and ability to float easily in the water.)

Kroeber sensed something out-of-the-ordinary in this use of flat tule leaves and he chided Bob for it. Bob sassed him--and Kroeber's notation in his notebook gives his reply. (It is still available to see in the notes in the Bancroft Library.) He said that Bob was garrulous and a bad informer, and he used other uncomplimentary epithets.

The result was that the songs Bob had recorded were evidently destroyed when they returned home. (Although it was never explained, it could be surmised that, with the flat tules, Bob was weaving a sail for the tule boat he was intending to make from round-stemmed tules. One would have to make the sail first so that it could be installed deep in the bundles of tules used in making the boat.)

So Kroeber failed to preserve Old Bob's songs. Fortunately, others did preserve them a few years later, as we shall see.

The Songs of Salt Lake Pete

After destroying the cylinders he had recently recorded of Bob's singing, Kroeber probably went to the Tule River Reservation near Porterville. There, he recorded more than 50 songs of Salt Lake Pete, the medicine man. That was Yaudanci territory. Pete's father was Yaudanci; his mother was Yokod, from Yokohl Valley. Pete sang in the Yaudanci-Yokuts dialect.[1]

Kroeber probably asked him if he knew any Tachi songs. Pete must have replied that he knew some, but suggested that he would like to talk to coyote first.

---

[1] The cassette copies of these and other songs recorded by Salt Lake Pete are available in the Lowie Museum Collection at U.C. Berkeley. They are known as the Kroeber recordings of 1903.

The Kroeber recordings were recently re-recorded onto cassette tapes and catalogued by Dr. Richard Keeling, who was until recently on the staff of U.C.L.A. in the Department of Ethnomusicology. The tapes begin with the recordings of Salt Lake Pete.

A large number of California Indian songs had been collected over the years, beginning in 1903 and were on tapes at the Lowie Museum in Berkeley, California. The California Indian Music Project (1983-1985), directed by Dr. Richard Keeling, was a project to copy the cassette tapes of the Indian songs and to return them to the Indian communities from which they came. The cassette tapes were also made available to students interested in studying them. The primary project was funded by the National Endowment for the Arts, the California Arts Council, and the L.J. and Mary C. Skaggs Foundation.

72

COYOTE SONG

Pete began the recording session with Coyote Song. Later came the amusing, exciting Lemoore Song in which he attempted to put the Mexican Dance music into the strait-jacket of the Indian 5-tone scale. Many of Pete's songs used only four tones or pitches. They are not always the same four tones, nor do they always have the same relationship to each other. If we knew the language, they would be more interesting to us. The words seem all-important. The songs usually have no noticeable form.

medicine man's hat

In Coyote Song, Pete is talking. Perhaps he is putting on his dance clothes as he speaks.[1] Professor Kroeber is in charge of the recording machine. Pete is talking in bits of sentences. We can make out the word, "Kaye", (Coyote). He is explaining something. He is calling Coyote. There is a tremelo in Pete's voice. He is amused. We hear a low, murmuring laugh. Is he calling Coyote? Or, is he changing himself into Coyote? This whole number takes three and a half minutes!

One can picture him skirmishing about, acting the part of the trickster, his shaggy tail swooping, his head twisting about, and his eyes furtively glancing to one side, and to the other side, looking for Coyote. One hears a bark and the hot breath of the animal--and one feels the presence of Coyote.

---

[1] The medicine man's dance clothes were, briefly, the eagle-down skirt, the cotton net covering the head topped with a circlet of eagle-down going around the head, and the hat, with magpie feathers encircling the brim, and road-runner feathers sticking straight up at the top of the hat. These clothes are not to be called a costume. They are dancing clothes.

The Lemoore Song & the Mexican Hat Dance

Another song on the cassette tape of Kroeber's recordings of Salt Lake Pete is called "The Lemoore Song." Lemoore is a town seven miles north of the Tachi Rancheria. When examined closely, the first two measures of the Lemoore song are strongly similar to those of the tune popularly known as the "Mexican Hat Dance." It is not too difficult to imagine how such similarity could have occurred:

We can imagine an Indian party in Lemoore where there are Mexicans present and where, to entertain the crowd, the visitors performed the Hat Dance. Perhaps there is music by fiddle and guitar. The Hat Dance is a flirtatious number, with the hat, a typical sombrero, worn by the gentleman, and the China Poblana costume worn by the woman. There is a dance step[1] to simulate the rhythm of a galloping horse. Nine tunes follow the first tune with variations in the dance of steps and skips. As for the hat, in the grand finale the man places it on the floor at the feet of his partner. If she accepts him, she dances around it, repeatedly touching her dainty foot inside the brim. Then she lifts the hat and, as the music describes it, she "picks it up and puts it on." Then the couple dances together for the whirlwind finale of the music.

The music and dance no doubt had an exhilarating effect on the crowd; and, as Salt Lake Pete was there, he too, may have been caught up in the enthusiasm of the moment. As a result he created a song with similar melody and rhythm but in the unmistakable Indian style. He felt compelled to put it in the familiar mode of the Indian music, and he allowed himself only the five-tone scale. The eight-tone scale was used in the Mexican dance tune.

---

[1] The dance step: a stamp by the left foot, and a heel-toe tap on the right foot, a transferring of weight on the right toe, and back to the left foot on the accent.

In the vicinity of Bakersfield, Mexicans were employed as vaqueros and "Mexican musicians often supplied music for the social affairs of the community," as early as 1870. In other places, Mexicans were raising fine fields of grain. There was a Mexican village called San Emigdio which stood on the plains between Kern Lake and Buena Vista Lake on the north and the mountains on the south. In 1870, it was announced that "two gentlemen with violin and harp were ready to respond to any call made upon them."[1] With such a background, it is possible that Mexicans with their music and dance would have visited the Tachis.

It was a considerable feat to adapt the melody, which was intended for instrumental music, to a melody that could be sung with Indian words. It reveals that Salt Lake Pete was a talented musician. As to the Indians who were at the party, they must thus have realized that there was "other music." They would never give up their own songs, their own style, and their own culture; but they could see in another's culture another way with music. Kroeber later paid another visit to Salt Lake Pete and asked him to repeat the "Lemoore Song." Evidently, he had noted the similarity of that song with the Mexican Hat Dance. But, Pete had forgotten how he had sung the song the first time. All that he remembered was the beginning rather high note was held, and that one he produced with a rush of enthusiasm; and, he remembered the provocative rhythm of a galloping horse.

The following analysis shows the basis for this probable external influence. Both of the tunes have been transcribed from the original key, so that they would begin on the same note, making it easier to compare the two.

---

[1] William Harland Boyd, *A California Middle Border: the Kern River Country*, 1772-1880. {Richardson, TX.} Havilah Press, 1972, p. 196.

THE MEXICAN HAT DANCE

Notice that there is a hold on an announcing chord, the F major chord, using the notes FACF. The key signature of B flat further identifies it as being in the key of F major. In the melody the outline of the F major chord is revealed in the first two measures. There are some other notes there which are not in the F chord, which are like ornaments on the framework of the F chord. These ornamental notes are neither F, A, or C. They are called bytones or affixes. A slash through the notes identifies the ones that are bytones.

The rest of the example given above outlines very neatly the scale of F major, beginning on the third note of that scale.

THE LEMOORE SONG

Notice the hold on the first note of the song in the Lemoore Song. It corresponds to the hold on the introductory chord in the Mexican Hat Dance. Pete evidently felt that he should use only tones allowable in other Indian songs--either four or five tones. He usually used only four tones in a song. This time he allowed himself five tones. He squeezed together the tones of the Mexican melody into a melody of five tones (with affixes). It is an odd tune, but it *is* Indian.

76

COYOTE DANCING SONG

Still another of Pete's songs collected by Kroeber was the
Coyote Dancing Song (different from the Coyote Song).

Sung by Salt Lake Pete

Catalogue #24-577   Recorded by A.L. Kroeber

The singer is finding his tones and at the same time is calling Coyote. The tones he is groping for are the familiar Coyote
tones:

C
B flat
G
F

In musical terms this cluster of tones is called a figure. It is a musical idea. These are the same set of tones that start the Coyote Song in the set of songs collected by Cummins. This Coyote Dancing Song is one of the songs recorded by Kroeber when he asked Salt Lake Pete, the Yaudanci Medicine Man, to sing for him. You will notice that the style of singing differs from that of Bob's, the Tachi medicine man. It is much more difficult to transcribe the songs of Pete because there seemingly is no plan, no form...no repeating section. Instead each tone seems to have an identity; as though the tones are all old friends.

Playing through the tapes of many of Pete's songs we find the same four tones or tones having the same relationship to each other or, an entirely different set of four tones. Five songs had three tones, three had four tones and one had five tones. Finding the differences in the songs of the two medicine men and noticing the one musical figure where their songs are alike (the Coyote figure), is the fascinating part of this kind of research. There is a tendency to rate the Yaudanci songs as less advanced than the Tachi because they are not like our European music, but I think we should not judge them. We should accept both kinds of songs.

Harrington's Collection

It was 13 years later when Harrington visited the Tachis, and he too recorded some of their songs.

His notes of that visit in 1916 show 32 songs. The transcriptions of them (music notes on paper) by Helen Roberts, number only 13.

Perhaps some of the cylinders were damaged or maybe there was never the time nor inclination to finish the difficult job.

J. P. Harrington
(Smithsonian Institution).

SLEEPY SONG

This is song No. 11 of Harrington's notes. Bob had told Harrington that when he danced, and it was getting to be daylight and everybody was sleepy; he sang this song and they woke up.

After the song, the crowd calls[1] with hand over mouth,.....then the sighing Ah...Ah....then the words, "more, more." The singers sing it over again.

---

[1] Calling: a sound frequently used by children and heard on TV or movies depicting a call by groups of Indians. They cover and uncover their mouths while producing an extended vowel sound. (They "pat" their mouths.)

Sleepy Song

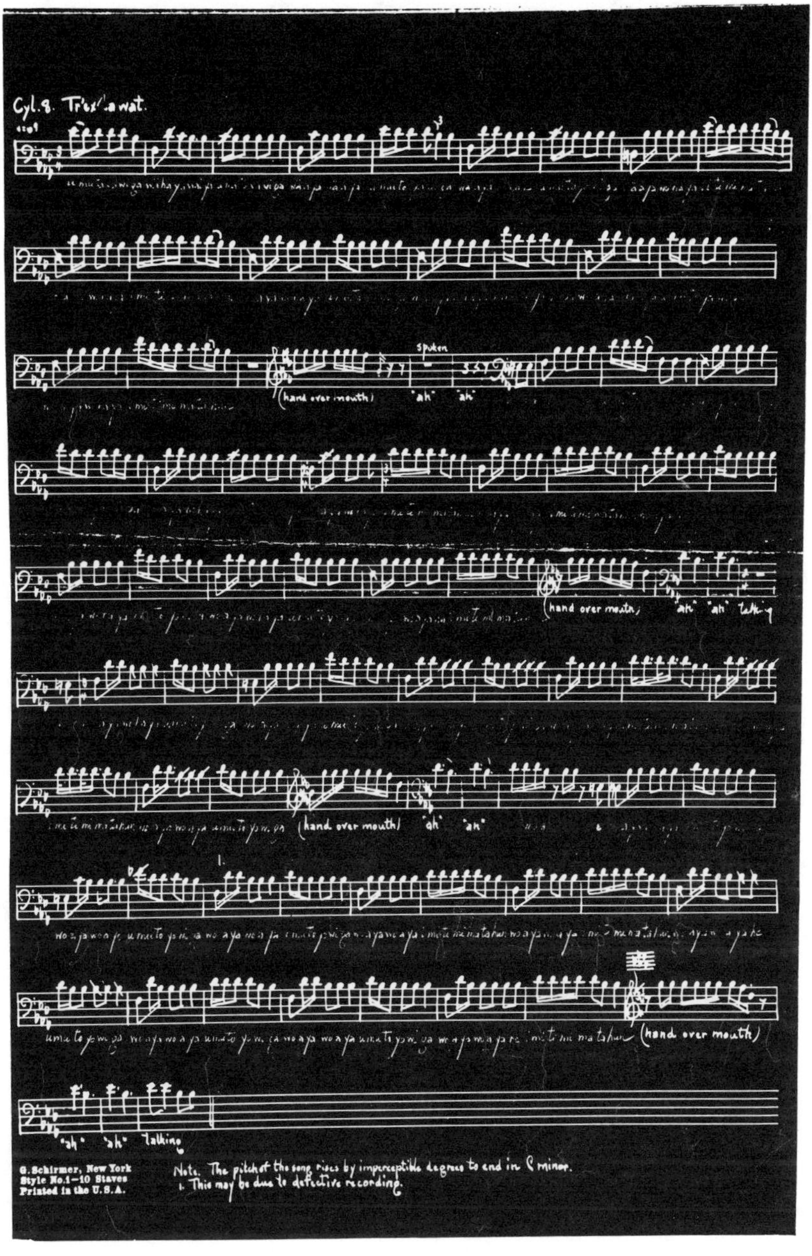
Cyl. 8. Tr'ex'ʔawat.
spoken
(hand over mouth)
"ah" "ah"
(hand over mouth)
"ah" "ah" talking
(hand over mouth)
"ah" "ah"
(hand over mouth)
"ah" "ah" talking
G. Schirmer, New York
Style No.1—10 Staves
Printed in the U.S.A.
Note. The pitch of the song rises by imperceptible degrees to end in C minor.
1. This may be due to defective recording.

Bob's Recording of Sleepy Song

The Words and their Meanings from Harrington's Notes

E wo a ya a ya   Umu tu yo wi ga   (sleepy) (too much, very)

Wo a ya wo a ya Umu tu yo wi ga   (sleepy) (o wi-ko too much very)

Wo a ya wo a ya Umu tu yo wi ga   (wo-aj a woja=sleepy) (too much, very)

Wo a ya wo a ya   (wo-aj a woja=sleepy) (too much, very)

* * * * * * * * * * *

I mi ti mi ma ta hun   (ma ta hun = to go up)

Wo aya wo a ya

I mi ti mi ma ta hun

Wo a ya wo a ya hi

* * * * * * * * * * *

Umu tu yo wi ga

Wo a ya wo a ya

U mu tu yo wi ga

Wo a ya wo a yahi

U mu tu yo wi ga Wo a ya wo a ya

I mi ti mi ma ta hun. . .

Then the crowd calls with hand over mouth. . . .then the sighing
Ah. . .Ah. . .then the words, "more, more."

82

Harrington originally recorded Bob's songs on old-fashioned cylinders, not on discs or tapes that we have now. He wrote notations about the songs (in Tachi), giving the words and what Bob said about them (in English) as they were recorded. The notes show 32 songs, the transcriptions that I own, made by Helen Roberts, show 13 songs. As you can see, there is a mismatch. Some songs in Harrington's are not in Roberts', and vice-versa. The songs originally on cylinders have been re-recorded on cassette tapes.

In 1940, Clarence Atwell, the Tachi Medicine Man at that time, gave the meaning of the song as, "Sleepiness goes up, it goes down, up, sleep no more," and he gestured with his arms, putting them down and then up above his head.

In 1985, a Tachi woman living at the rancheria said, "I sing that song, but I never really thought of the words."

Clarence Atwell in 1940

Harrington's notes, the Helen Roberts' transcriptions into music notation, and six cassette tapes were donated to the Kings County Library in the summer of 1990. It is hoped that they will be found and studied by persons who will appreciate them. I am sure J.P. Harrington would be pleased if he knew that these songs were added to the repertoire of the chorus at the Tachi Rancheria. The Tachis have been my friends for 50 years. It is time now to pass on these materials to someone else.

Helen Roberts' Collection

Miss Helen Roberts, who previously had transcribed Harrington's recordings onto music paper, came to the Tachi rancheria herself in 1925. She gathered 94 songs from Old Bob, (the medicine man, Roberto Bautista) and she gathered 1,500 songs from the north to the south in the far west.

I searched by telephone for these recordings to Yale University Library, to the Lowie museum, University of California at Berkeley, to the Library of Congress, and to the Folk Life Center of the Library of Congress but eventually had to give up the project--still empty handed. Finally I decided that there were no recordings. Miss Roberts was very capable of transcribing the songs to music paper directly as they were being sung, especially if the singer were willing to repeat his singing as many times as needed.

Finally, I sent off a letter to the Folk Life Center and enclosed a copy of the letter sent to me from Miss Roberts in 1940. That did it. The lady at the Folk Life Center found two black notebooks where Miss Roberts had written the notes, words, meanings and comments of Old Bob, Tachi-Yokuts medicine man, singer of the songs in 1925. Miss Roberts despaired of this interesting material ever being published because of the expense and the small public interest. She did not foresee the days of the copier and the computer.

Helen Roberts died at the age of 97 in 1986.

HELEN H. ROBERTS
HIGH WATCH
TRYON
NORTH CAROLINA

Aug. 22 1940.

Miss Marjorie E. Whited
Crockett, Kings County,
Calif.

My dear Miss Whited:-

I have your letter regarding the music and dances of the Tachi tribe of Yokuts Indians. My notes are at present quite inaccessible and after a lapse of many years I am without them not absolutely certain that the Indians I worked with at Lemoore were Tachi but I am almost sure they were. From Old Bob alone, I got more than 100 songs (no, 95 from him) and there were several other informants and Mr. J. P. Harrington of the Smithsonian Institution in Washington gathered great masses of ethnological data, including dances and many fine photographs. In fact, he literally combed California in 1920 - 23 or even until nearly 1930 - and I doubt if there was an Indian in the state worth seeing that escaped intensive work with him. I myself gathered some 1500 songs or more from

the north to the south, tho I did not cover everything as he did. These have never been published though all the records have been transcribed. The cost of publishing studies like these is prohibitive in view of the limited interested reading public. I doubt if anything has been published from this region, certainly nothing of any moment.

Very truly yours
Helen H. Roberts.

Personal letter to the author in 1940, written by Helen Roberts.

THE LIBRARY OF CONGRESS

WASHINGTON, D.C. 20540

AMERICAN FOLKLIFE CENTER

March 1, 1990

Dear Ms. Cummins:

In response to your inquiry, yes, we do have Helen Roberts's transcription notebooks containing songs by Bob Bautista (Trex'Lawat). Sixteen pages in one notebook contain the transcriptions made in November-December, 1922, of fourteen songs on eleven cylinders recorded by Harrington. We have those eleven cylinders in our collection; I am enclosing our cataloging information on those eleven cylinders, now listed as part of the J.P. and Carobeth Harrington Southern Valley Yokuts collection (these pages will be part of volume five of the Federal Cylinder Project catalog series, now in the publishing office and due to be out later this year).

The additional ninety-four songs, to which Roberts referred in her letter to you, are in two other notebooks. To my knowledge, Roberts did not record them on cylinders but, as you surmised, took them down by dictation. The transcriptions are in pencil; some are quite difficult to read at this point. The musical notation is on one page, with additional notes on the facing page in some cases. I count sixty-seven pages with notation and commentary.

If you are interested in obtaining photocopies of this material, please write to the Library's Photoduplication Service (see the enclosed information sheet) for an order form and procedures. Current fees are forty-five cents per page plus shipping. You would need to tell them to contact me at extension 7-1740 in order to get the notebooks.

I hope this information will be helpful.

Sincerely,

Judith A. Gray
Federal Cylinder Project

Ms. Marjorie W. Cummins
2064 Carter Way
Hanford, CA 93230

The Cummins Collection

I was given the 78 rpm phonograph record containing 10 Tachi songs made about a week before the pow-wow of March 1, 1940. The singers had been practicing for several weeks under the leadership of Clarence Atwell, who would become the new medicine man.

The recording was especially good. There was no distracting sound of the machine's motor; each song was clear, and each was announced by Jack Robinson, the owner of the recording machine.

The ten songs have since been put on cassette tapes and given to Clarence Atwell, Jr.

Sleepy Song, Tachi Coyote Song and Eagle Song are discussed here. The others were Mahogony Tree Song, Indian Tobacco Song, Deer Song, Women's Hand Game Song, Men's Hand Game Song, Rain Song, and Burris Park Song.

SLEEPY SONG

This was the same song recorded by Harrington 24 years earlier. By the time it was recorded in 1940, the Tachis had found another use for the song. They used it to put everyone back to sleep if they had wakened in the night. Here is an imaginative sketch of how it might have been in the days when they lived in tule huts long before 1940.

Can you imagine how it was, living in a house made of reeds? How at night the wind would whisper and whistle through the walls? The rain would beat a soft tattoo on the layers of dried tules. Safe inside and snug under their rabbit skin covers, the Indians would draw closer together. Someone would put another stick or two on the coals at the center and some little flames would throw long flickering shadows on the walls. The mothers would hold their children close to them under the warm robes and they would sing this song. It was meant to be sung softly to help everyone go back to sleep.

Sleepy Song
Recording by Jack Robinson
Transcription by M. Cummins

Sung by Josie Atwell, Bessie Brunell, Belle Mendosa in 1940.

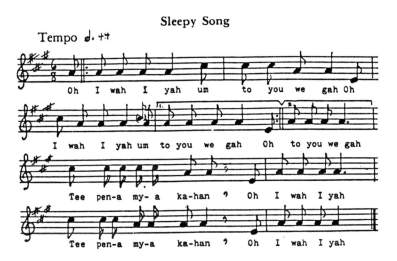

Oh I wah I yah
Um to you we gah
Tee pen-a my-a ka-han
Oh I wah I yah.

TACHI COYOTE SONG
(1940)

The melody of the first part of this Coyote Song, is descriptive of the wanderings of Coyote, himself. The melody starts "up there somewhere" (a medium high note) and trends downward in small steps and skips in an uncertain manner. It represents Coyote, benignly and intriguingly wandering along without any destination. But, in truth, he is aware that close by there is a nice, fat rabbit.

In the second half of the tune, the howl of coyote is simulated very cleverly in the melody. Many nights, the Indian who dreamed this song must have heard the distant howl of the coyote as he gave his call to the moon over the lake. The animal would raise his voice, and then raise it a bit higher in an effort to reach that bright thing in the sky. And he would try again, lifting, lifting, never reaching, and then letting his voice trail off into the darkness of the water below.

This is not the same as Pete's Coyote Song except for the four note "figure" for Coyote.

Could it be that this one was Coyote himself, the One with supernatural powers, the clown and the trickster who could vanish and appear again at some distances away? The rise and fall of the melody was patterned after the rise and fall of Coyote's howl.

Coyote Song

(Ka-Ye)

Tempo ♩ = 132

Rattle rhythm ♩♩♩♩ except where trill is marked

Ee way taw nem nah ne-ma toe ho ne-na

Ee way taw nem nah ne-ma toe ho ne-na

How we he ma-nan, Mo-he lee ma - ha-na

Ka-ye we ma -ha — na-na

EAGLE SONG
(1940)

This song was dreamed. Clarence had asked the elders of the tribe for permission to be their medicine man. When the request was granted, he set out to find his song.

He went over to the western hills. He laid down and was soon overcome with sleep. When he awoke he saw an eagle standing on a rock close by, and then he remembered the song that had come to him in his dream. It was a song about Eagle. Eagle represented strength, the undisputed leader, the supreme wise one.

Ralph Powell and The Hanford Sentinel
A Tachi dance in 1940 by Medicine Man,
Clarence Atwell facing his mother, Josie Atwell.

The man was Clarence Atwell. He did become the medicine man. He revived the old custom of having a pow-pow on March first, and he trained a group of singers to sing again the songs that they had almost forgotten. On March first he wore the customary regalia of a Tachi-Yokuts medicine man made by his mother, Josie Atwell. Other Indians had been invited too, and they had a pow-wow. It was like in the old days when Old Bob was their medicine man and the singing of the old songs revived their spirits and warmed their hearts. Clarence danced and sang the Eagle Song. He

92

waved his swatch of feathers over a sick, old woman to heal her, as tears ran down her cheeks. Another woman threw handfulls of seeds on the fire. The crackling of the burning seeds was a way of protecting them from illness "that might catch up with them".

The songs were a strong influence on the lives of the Yokuts Indians.

Eagle Song

"You Eagle that come to me,
Eagle, come over,
Fly around *me* once or twice."

Tempo ♩ = 132

Rattle ♩♩♩♩ except where trill is marked over the notes

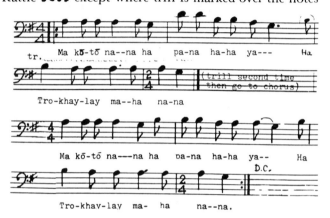

Chorus

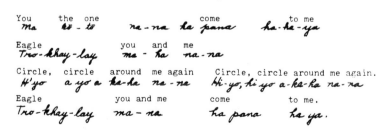

Mission Influence

One wonders how much the songs had been influenced by the music heard at the missions. Anything that came to their ears in the way of music would have had an influence, no matter how small. The intoning of Mass when the missionary priest, accompanied by soldiers, came in search of converts, would have opened their ears to new ways of singing. And, did the Spanish soldiers sing Spanish folk songs around the fire at night?

Some of the missions had choirs composed partly of Indians, the music written on large sheets of parchment, one copy used for all; and in a few missions the friars had the patience to teach simple music for the violin, or the flute, or the cornet. Mission San Juan Bautista had a mission band. At the pueblos there was Spanish music: folk songs and dances like Varsovien, and later, Mexican music--fandangos, folk songs accompanied by guitar, and so on. To sum up: European music had been brought to the new world and was here in Coastal California, but the outlanders, the Indians of the interior, did not adopt it and continued with their own songs, in their own idiom. We see this in the number three song, the Lemoore Song of Salt Lake Pete, where, in my belief, he has heard the Mexican Hat Dance, Jarabe Tapatio, in which the first phrase was built on the tonic chord (but Pete reduced it to a figure in his own five-tone scale.)

Flutes

The Author Hears a Song from the Plains of MiddleAmerica

One afternoon, in 1983, I saw a group of Indians sitting on the lawn outside of the school building at the rancheria. I could tell that something unusual was happening. I could see a number of adults sitting or working at a table; there were quite a few children--boys dressed in Indian clothes with feathers in their hair--and some men sitting around an enormous drum.

There were men visiting that day from the Tule River Indian Reservation across the valley above Porterville. It is the home today of Indians from at least 32 other tribes, some of them from the plains of middle America.

I knew these men were not Yokuts, because Yokuts do not have drums.[1] I walked over to the scene of activity and was kindly invited to join them. They were having a birthday party for two of the children.

Each man sitting around the drum had a beater, a stick with a bulb of material on the end. At a signal, one man began a song that started with a shout on a high pitch (falsetto) and all commenced beating on the drum, in time. In the Indian language, he seemingly proclaimed some wrongful circumstance. As the melody cascaded downward, each portion of the breath spent its burden on a lower pitch than the one before, the stanza ended with these words sung in English, "the way of the BIA." As he sang these words his face turned up to disclose an expression of extreme frustration and misery. These were men who inherited this style of singing from the Indians of the great plains. It was a tumbling strain that Bruno Nettl wrote about. He had named this style as one of the possible developments that came after the really primitive "one-sustained-pitch" style.

---

[1] They used a foot drum made from a hollow log split in half lengthwise, placed on a slight depression in the ground, concave side uppermost, stomped on with the foot, or pounded with a long pole, the drummer standing upright.

I know little about the BIA (Bureau of Indian Affairs), but I do know that the Indians often felt that its rulings were not sympathetic to their needs. However, I thought this was no time to discuss a sore subject. Yokuts-type songs soon commenced and the boys danced to them in a circle, feet flying. They enjoyed it, and the birthday party was a success--potato salad, beans, cake, and all.

In Memoriam of 1940

Yoimut, that remarkable Indian woman born in 1855, who knew a great deal about Indian ways, died in 1937.[1] Old Bob, the medicine man, had died a few years earlier.

Since 1940, when the Tachis had a pow-wow at the Santa Rosa Rancheria, the memories of the old culture, its language, its social structure, its chief and shaman, its early foods, its songs and the seasonal festivities are less and less remembered. Robert Heizer, professor of anthropology at the University of California at Berkeley, summed it up in 1979, by writing:

"Memories, progressively dimmer, of the old original way of life survived among some (Indian) groups in California until about 1940. By that date the ethnographic record was as nearly complete as it was ever to be."[2]

Al Pietroforte

Josie Atwell, mother of Medicine Man, Clarence Atwell, in 1940

---

[1] Frank F. Latta, *Handbook of the Yokuts Indians*, Bear State Books, 1977, pp. 667-730.

[2] Robert F. Heizer, *Handbook of North American Indians: California*, Washington D.C.: Smithsonian Institution, 1978, p. 32.

To the happy group that made the recording of songs in 1940, sadness came in later years. Clarence, the medicine man, brought a new and younger wife to the Rancheria to live in a cabin next to his mother, Josie, and Christine, wife number one, and their two children. (Christine was twenty years his senior). They say it takes 15 years for a medicine man to perfect his powers, but with Clarence Atwell who became medicine man in 1940, those years were cut short when both he and his new wife died in 1948. Josie took care of the new baby, a son, Clarence Atwell, Jr., who is now tribal chairman. Thomas P. Thomas and his companion, Mike Sisco, were killed when their car collided with a train in 1958.

John Brunell, who played the fiddle for their dancing parties, died in 1953. Josie died in 1962 and Jim Brunell passed away in 1969. Belle, Yoimut's daughter, died at a rest home in Hanford in 1975. Bessie Brunell, the youngest of the group in 1940, died at the Rancheria in 1987.

These Tachis recorded songs in 1940. They were (L-R), Thomap P. Thomas, John Brunell, Clarence Atwell, Bessie Brunell, Jim Brunell, Nick Sisco, Josie Atwell and Belle Mendoza.

World War II began in December of 1941 and with it the Yokuts' world was greatly changed. No one's life was ever the same after that. Some left the rancheria and reservation to live in towns and cities where they found jobs; some enlisted.

This author, married and went to another state. Twins were born and from that time on her work was laid out for her.

Frank Baga returned to the rancheria with a Silver Star and a Purple Heart. The status of Indians went up. The status of tribes escalated some. In the time of President Reagan (1980s) the status of the tribe became that of a "nation within a nation".

In spite of all, the songs the singers knew in those early days were not destined to die, but were saved by the cooperation of both whites and Indians and the little cassette tapes.

Basketry

Indian basketry was almost entirely the work of the Indian woman. She needed baskets to gather, process, and cook her food. But there was much more to the making of a basket than its strictly utilitarian purpose. The artistic impulse that led to the creation of a basket (its shape, size, color, and pattern) revealed the Indian woman's inner life.

It was her poem because it displayed in a material way the caring and affection for those it

Rosie Baga, born in 1911 in a tule hut on the Kings River, carried on the tradition of making beautiful Yokuts bnaskets.

was to serve; it was her painting because she set the design and color in graceful proportion; it was her sculpture because she shaped the traditional form for the intended use; it was her cathedral because she adhered to the rules of basketry, its symbols and meanings; it was her music because she stitched or wove the rhythmic pattern she had chosen.

Basketry was a skill learned in childhood to the degree that a girl was able to complete her first basket at the age of five. The mother would teach her daughter the places to gather materials and the season to gather them. The preparation of the roots was begun by scraping and splitting them to a uniform size and then making them into rolls for storage. It was all a long process from beginning to the finished basket. When she had acquired the skill, she was ready to choose the form and the design. When she had determined these, she wove or stitched the basket in all of her spare time in the next three to eight months.

While the Yokuts culture had little of the arts except the music and the myth, the Yokuts Indian woman fulfilled her yearning for artistic expression in her basketry, which she elevated to an art.

The stiff figures of men and women sometimes seen on baskets made by California Indians are variations made to please American settlers. Whenever one sees such a design, one knows that it was influenced by the white man's culture and is not "for real". The Yokuts baskets had poise and restraint in design and were simple and perfect in execution. No one would need to apologize for their expression of the art. In fact, if they were to be called "Digger Indians," in a derogatory way, the skill and artistry in this regard glorified that name.

We should not feel that the Yokuts culture was lacking in richness, depth, or originality. The Yokuts had no wood carvings, no ceremonial artifacts, no manufactured jewelry set with semi-precious stones (an art learned from their Spanish conquerors by the Indians of the southwest), no masks and colorful costumes and no corn dances. What they did have were myths told at the fireside and lost when no longer needed. And they had songs sung on the air, ending with the click of a split-stick rattle, and vanishing in the wind. There were ceremonies performed for the day and the season. Then they were gone until the next season. All was unrecorded.

One Indian woman of another tribe found a way of recording a legend to reinforce her memory of the tale. It was by making a basket and putting symbols in the design representing the events of that legend. She saw a need and she invented a way. It was like the beginning of picture writing, as happened long ago with the Egyptians. The legend of "The Peopling of California," as illustrated in a basket, and told by a Sabobas Indian woman of Southern California, is related on page 63.

There came later, people of another race, products of thousands of years of work in the saving of precious events of their own race. They saved these memorable events through writing, through printing, and eventually through recording instruments. They saved them through pictures -- through colored pictures -- through moving pictures. They recorded the songs on cylinder, on disc, on cassette; and later, both songs and pictures together were recorded on videotape.

To these other people, this Indian culture was repeating the story of their own culture begun in far distant lands: in Europe, Asia, Northern Africa, and other places, thousands of years before. An understanding of the cultures of the Native Americans was necessary for them to better understand their own culture, to know what they had gained and what they had lost, and to interpret the present.

The Yokuts' Religion

The history of California Indians, scientists generally agree, goes back to 10,000 years ago or at the time when the last ice age was beginning to lose its hold. The wave of immigration from Siberia at that time peopled the western and southwestern areas of North America and eventually spread out to all of North, Central and South America. They brought their languages with them and what culture had suited their very cold climate in the extreme north. Further waves of migration are supposed to have taken place 6,000 years ago from Siberia and 4,000 years ago from Northern Asia. And so, the Indians of California and other areas as well, had many thousands of years to develop a culture, a religion and a society with a political structure to enable them to live at peace with each other. As far as we know, they had no Messiah such as the Caucasians of Western Europe had nor a prophet such as Mohammad in Islam. There was no Buddha as in India. But through ceremony-sharing (called Ceremonialism), they developed a religion. They were highly successful builders of a society.

The aim of most Indians was not that of acquiring wealth. Lack of accumulated wealth prevented the development of hereditary social classes, which some think eventually leads to an authoritarian type of government. Only the leader could acquire wealth, and that through donations as he must have enough to give away to those in need. Today, as in the past, everyone has a voice and a vote in the Indian social and political structure. (That is why meetings drag on and on until there is 100% agreement.)

Native Californians thought of themselves not as individuals operating independently, but as part of the group, the tribe, interrelated to the animals and plants and all included as part of the environment--a true community encompassing all. This philosophy is part of the religious experience of the people. While they have day-to-day dealings with reality, they believe in a mystical level, a realm of dreams and visions, into which they can enter and establish connections with the sources of power.

Power

The power of the forces of nature is obvious to any who live close to nature and to any who satisfy all of their needs from nature. If you stand at the side of a river as it plunges down to a lower level, the deafening sound of it tells us there is **power** there. Native Americans looked toward such phenomena with personal interaction through dreams, visions, ceremonies, and intuitive ways of controlling those forces.

Ceremonies imparted a visual expression of what they believed and made it possible for people to have a sense of **power** over their environment. Thus the Rain Song was believed to ensure the right amount of rain for the season when sung with the right ceremonies; the flower festival promised the colors of the rainbow and the production of seeds for the seed gathering in the fall.

The performing of ceremonies was a part of their religious beliefs, and practicing these rites, they could appeal to the forces of nature that manifested the **power**.

Some of this philosophy and these beliefs they may have brought with them from the regions of northern Asia and Siberia where shamanism was, and still is, practiced over a larger area than at any other place in the world. They were mainly the hunters of animals in their place of origin. But as they came into this warmer climate and the changed environment, these primal folk added the gathering of plants to their hunting of animals, and probably the stories they told to interpret the mysteries of life changed, too.

Before 1772, the Yokuts lived in Indian communities in which nearly every act had religious and moral significance and a song to express it. However, after the appearance of the white man, in many cases, the negative self-image appeared as a result of the low opinion many white people had of them. The term "Digger Indians" designated them as inferior and contributed to their feeling of inferiority.[1]

The great world religions today, judged by the number of followers each has, are Christianity, Muslim, and Buddhism. Each of these has its origin in the teachings of a founder, each has apostles, priests, or special disciples, and each has its wisdom preserved in books and writings. But, with the Indians, no great

---

[1] These opinions are expressed in the book by James J. Rawls , titled *Indians of California*, Univ. of Oklahoma Press, Norman, OK, 1984.

teacher had appeared--as yet. The combination of their culture and ceremonies, their shamanism and dreams, and their kinship with nature, constituted a belief system--a religion. The songs and dances, the legends and myths, yes, and the rock paintings, were all a part of it. The shaman received revelations in a dream state, a state which opened the channel to the subconscious mind shared by all humans.

At the present time Native Americans are not looking to whites for guidance in the saving of outward aspects of their religion, such as songs and myths. It is for whites themselves that these arts are saved, that we may know what a complex, worthwhile, and interesting culture we have so nearly destroyed. The non-Native American will not only find this culture interesting, but knowledge of it will help in the understanding of his own past and in the prediction of his future.

THE YOKUTS' PRAYER

*For as man was possessed of a soul, a spirit, so were all
animals and plants, all created matter. And within all matter was
power, power for good - and for evil....And there was magic.*

The Yokuts Prayer is from Kroeber's book.[1] In his notes, now
in the Bancroft Library, he wrote that he was there and heard it given
before a gathering of Yaulemani-Yokuts (who lived in the southern
part of the valley, east of Bakersfield). The reader may assume that
Kroeber took the Indian aside afterwards and asked him to repeat
the prayer, that he had the help of an interpreter, and that he took
careful notes.

The reader may be shocked as I was that these Yokuts were
appealing to strange gods. Kroeber explains that they lived near
other tribes who were not Yokuts. The Gabrielinos (from San
Gabriel Mission, northeast of Los Angeles), the Kiwaiisus (in the
hills to the Yokuts'south, facing the Mojave Desert), the Fernandenos,
(from the San Fernando Mission) in a valley north of Los Angeles,
and the Serranos (northeast of San Diego)--those Indians all had
gods. The Yaulemanis did not want to be left out of any good
fortune that might take place, and so they petitioned the gods of their
neighbors. They borrowed their gods.

Tribes living in proximity often borrowed from each other,
borrowed almost everything: songs, myths, ceremonies, games --
and gods. The names of some of those divinities were titles given
to revered chieftains of great power and influence - but some were
really gods to the Indians. This was a counter-religion. Perhaps it
was meant to provide an alternative to the religion brought in by a
foreign power, represented by priests in odd clothing and who
practiced with strange symbols and spoke a foreign language.

---

[1] Alfred L. Kroeber, *Handbook of the Indians of California*; Washington:
Government Printing Office, 1925, pp.511 and 623.

The names of the gods in this prayer were Indian, they were near at hand, and perhaps sometimes they even lived in the valley.

And what a prayer it was! Kroeber wrote that the prayer was intoned, that is, it was spoken on a singing tone--as the priest does in the Catholic service at times. It was a prayer conceived on a grand scale.

Man is a supplicant in need of help. He appeals to the great ones, the powerful ones, to see him, defenseless, an Indian with a plea for help. It is an appeal to the power of the great mountains, the great rocks, and the great trees. He is one with them. The words he speaks are connected with the great power manifestations of nature; they are the articulating link with power. He has nothing to fear from Day and Night because he is one with the whole world.

The Yaulumne-Yokuts Prayer

Do you see me!
See me, Tuushiut!
See me, Pamashiut!
See me, Yuhahait!
See me, Echepat!
See me, Pitsuriut!
See me, Tsukit!
See me, Ukat!
Do you all help me!

My words are tied in one
With the great mountains,
With the great rocks,
With the great trees,
In one with my body
And my heart.
Do you all help me
With supernatural power,

And you, Day,
And you, Night!
all of you see me,
One with this world!

The Veil

Old Bob was a medicine man when the old grandmother was young. The old woman, her three granddaughters, and a white woman were speaking in conversational tones, one day.

The query came, "Did you ever go to Old Bob when you were sick?"

Suddenly . . . .
came a voice, - a low-pitched, strong, strange voice, full of fear, yet fired with belief. It could have been heard above the icy wind of the northern wastes, the barren, treeless wastes of the Arctic. It was a command, indestructible in time, in hundreds of generations.

"He had the Power!"

It came again-- inescapable - "He Had the Power. Do you hear that, girls?" And the facetious talk and giggles of her granddaughters suddenly ceased. There was a serious silence.

The white woman looked down at the upturned face of one of the girls. There was no spoken word, but the expression on her face said something. It said, "We are afraid of our grandmother when she talks like this. What will you think of us? Will you think our grandmother is out of her mind? We have to believe this--we are Indians."

The veil that hung between the white woman and the Indians had been pierced. The secrets, the mystic, and the supernatural had been part of the old one's life, and now she was passing it on to the younger members of the tribe. The Yokuts' religion came with them across the arctic wastes.

An Indian Believes

Brown Wilson sat in the backyard of his Hanford home under the old grape arbor. He was surrounded by bales of junk and articles which had been useful at one time. Now they awaited just the right customer. There were lengths of pipe, some glass bottles, a piece of crockery that matched something long ago held dear, part of an old wagon, an anvil used in a blacksmith shop, and more.

While he was talking he was fondly handling a weathered oak limb, forked at the end, which he thought would make a good cradleboard and had been saved for that purpose. The Yokuts baby would be laid on a platform woven strongly and stretched tightly between the two forks of the limb, then the baby would be laced in with leather thongs or milkweed twine to hold him securely. Each cradle had a sunshade attached to it. A straight line pattern on the shade indicated the baby to be a boy; a wavy-like pattern would indicate a girl (perhaps because there were more curves in the feminine figure).

The following, which I have called An Indian Believes, came from an interview recorded on cassette tape by the author. It seems to be a mixture of philosophy and religion, both with strong Indian overtones.

Anything you believe, you must believe in it.
If you don' believe, it ain't gonna work.
It won't do you no good 'tall

And that's what our Lord told the people.
"If you don't believe in me, your day will be night."

You'll be out around in the night;
Daytime you will sleep.
And when you die, you'll go there and you'll go there....

"co-le-wit", the deep sloughs ...
That's where all the people that didn't believe go.

They'll always stay in this world.
Their soul is dead,
They'll never go to heaven, never.
They'll always stay in this world.

But if you go to heaven, your soul goes to it.
But you'll be born again.
You're gonna come back -- born again.

When woman pregnant, have to be very careful.
Don't look at that person and say,
"I don't like that person."
Don't try to talk to people.
Don't talk and say, "I don't like that person."

All along that river they've got poison oak.
White people had girl, got poison oak.
Indian doctor went out near Huron - got plant.

Then made fire and got ashes.
Took clothes off. . . . all over.
About twenty minutes started cool off.
In an hour looked all right.
It is not sage brush but looks like sage brush.
Smoke tree has power (oak tree)
They claim the baby will live long life.
You cure the tree right, put it in the shade.
You can move it in any direction.
(Co-rel' means papoose cradle).
Cut it in the right side of the moon.

Say, "I'm gon' make it, baby will make it."
When he grow up, put him on it every day.
Baby got a power .. be a strong man.
Nothing ain't gonna break him.

That's what the Indians think.
Its got long power.
'Cause it's raised by this thing {this cradle}.
That's what they believe.
As the baby grows, he's gon' to have power
as long as he lives.

You must believe in it,
. . . or if you don't believe, don't try.
That's what our Lord said,
"If you believe in me, your day will be Day.
If you don't believe in me, your day will be Night.

CHAPTER V

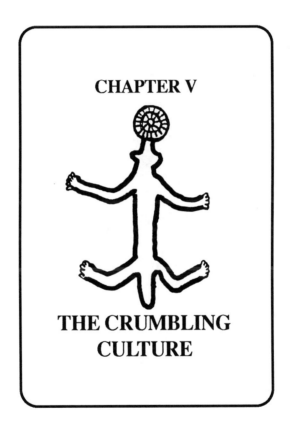

THE CRUMBLING
CULTURE

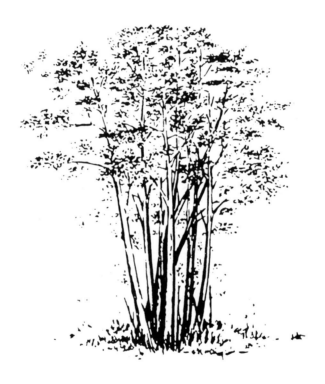

The Crumbling Culture

It was a land undespoiled. No tool heavier than a woman's digging stick had broken the earth's protective crust. Man was supplied by nature with a bounty of food and materials: nuts, berries, seeds, bulbs, leaves, fish, fowl, game, grasses for baskets, feathers, and hides---the list is endless. Between the land and its people, harmony had been developed; man taking in moderation, knowledgably and respectfully; man containing the population of his own species within numbers the natural garden could support.

Even though swept into the 19th and 20th centuries from primitive living, they still clung tenaciously to old customs, old ways. Yet, slowly the old ways did vanish. The songs and myths were forgotten. The story is inevitably sad because it is the story of dying, vanishing, and forgetting.

Along the coast, missions were built beginning in 1769; and the coastal Indians helped to build them. The men learned to tend fields and herd cattle and the women learned to do household chores besides learning about a new religion. There soon came into this valley runaways from those missions, fleeing because of the strict discipline or because they were homesick for tribal life. Then priests came seeking the runaways and trying to find new converts.

Father Martin`, a priest from San Miguel Mission in the Salinas Valley, came to the edge of the valley to the Cholam`es tribe in 1804. He wanted the Indian mothers to give him their children, saying they would always have enough to eat, something to wear, and, after a life of working for the church, they would go to a beautiful heaven.

Then the Indian chief came! He realized what the priest was about to do, he acted queerly and in an outrageous way. The mothers withdrew their children and all disappeared.

In a few days, soldiers came and escorted the chief and his son to San Miguel. The son was held hostage while the chief returned home to collect the many deer skins that had been exacted.

From that time on, nearly every year a priest came from one of the coastal missions. Children and the very old would be baptised. The others would be told that they would have to wait until a mission could be built in the valley.

Before long, trappers entered the valley. They came peacefully enough, but they were probably responsible for the great plague of 1833. Often the provincial governors of California sent out soldiers to explore and to find a site for a mission or a place for a fort. Something had to be done. The Yokuts were stealing horses from coastal settlers and bringing them into the valley, even across the valley... and eating them... or the Indians were herding horses into the valley and out on its southeastern side, through passes into the desert beyond, to the Santa Fe Trail where fresh mounts brought good prices. Such practices upset the whole Yokuts economy besides bringing reprisal from coastal ranchers. At that point, according to what few reports we have for evidence, the confusion became bloody and utterly degrading.

Some stray visitors came from France, South America and probably Russia. Then came the deluge of miners sweeping across the northern part of the valley to the gold fields destroying all that was in their way. Lastly, the settlers came into the valley starting about 1850. These opportunists were mostly of European stock. They brought diseases to which they were fairly immune, but to which the Indian had no immunity at all. Diseases . . . . guns . . . . liquor.

The Yokuts' lives had been so peaceful before the arrival of these strangers. The Indians told of no wars; there was no joining together in groups to defend their territory. Scientists think that since there was plenty of natural food for the taking, there was no need for them to fight for territory, no need to learn how to make war.

Among the Yokuts, and within the family, sharing was the rule, and selfishness was not countenanced. Morals were taught. In the male, bravery, fortitude, generosity, and wisdom were counseled;

in the female, industry, kindness and chastity were expected. The strength of the tribe resided in the individual families.[1] They saw the white man as both selfish and greedy--a cheater. They thought he would take advantage of the Indian in any agreement reached between them. The aggressiveness of the whites in acquiring property, accumulating materials, and in passing it on to their heirs, was foreign to the Yokuts' concept of right living.

Estanislao and Jedediah Smith

One Indian of outstanding intelligence who was trained at San Jose Mission and given responsibilities, ran away to the northern part of the San Joaquin Valley to set up a republic of his own. (His name, Estanislao, was later briefed and given to the river and county - Stanislaus - by the Americans). Estanislao held sway, looting, burning, and killing from 1825 until 1829, when General Mariano Guadalupe Vallejo, fresh from a victory over the Indians near Tulare Lake with cavalry, infantry, and artillery, came to subdue him.[1] The General was victorious and the Indians were destroyed. But Estanislao escaped. He fled to San Jose and asked Father Duran to forgive him and there he filled out his days in peace, a sadder but wiser man.

About that time, Jedediah Smith, a bible-toting trapper came into the valley. He came without permission from the California authorities or any letter from his own country seeking entry and giving his purpose in coming. He tried to explain to Governor Echeandia why he and 16 other heavily armed Americans were in the province in San Gabriel without permission. What he received was permission to return to the United States. However, instead of

---

[1] Anna B. Gayton, *Yokuts and Mono Chiefs and Shamans*, {NY:Kraus Reprint Corp., 1965: Reprint, Berkeley, CA: University of California Press, 1930).

returning by the most direct route, he returned by way of the San Joaquin Valley. He then became the first man from the United States to make an entry overland into California and the first white man, as we shall see, to cross the Sierra.[1]

They camped on the Stanislaus River with a huge pile of furs but without many necessities. They could not go to the coast because they would have been arrested, so Smith decided to cross the Sierra to report to the rendezvous with the other trappers near Salt Lake.

Returning, Smith was attacked by Mojave Indians who stole his supplies and he fled to San Gabriel Mission. There at the mission, Father Sanchez re-supplied him and he transported them finally to his destitute men camped on the Stanislaus. Smith then visited Father Duran at San Jose, Governor Echeandea at Monterey, and a Yankee skipper who went his bond, and he then received a permit to continue on north with his men to the Columbia River. There he sold his immense pile of furs for $20,000, a good sum, especially in those days.

Another man named Smith was an early visitor to the valley. This one went by the name of Peg-leg Smith. He was a rough character; but then, those were rough times. An Indian had shot him in the ankle. He replied with another shot--and the Indian lay dead. Then he begged his companions to cut off his leg because the shot had caused a jagged wound that he knew would not heal. None had the courage to help him so he undertook to do it himself. He took a sharp knife and cut the wound across evenly. Luckily the bleeding stopped and his companions carried him in a litter 150 miles to a Utah village where some Indian women nursed him back to health. Meantime, he carved himself a stump out of a sapling oak, and whittled it to size. He emerged in the spring with the stump for a leg. That was in 1829.

---

[1] Carl Briggs and Clyde Francis Trudell; *Quarterdeck and Saddlehorn, the Story of Edward F. Beale, 1822 - 1893*, Glendale, CA: A. H. Clark Co., 1983.

George H. Derby

George H. Derby, a topographical engineer, made a long exploratory tour of the southern part of the San Joaquin Valley in 1850. He later became identified with the San Francisco Herald, where he was the Will Rogers of the period, writing humorous sketches. He left Mission San Miguel in the Salinas Valley and, arriving at the San Joaquin Valley, he saw Tulare Lake spread out before him.

He approached the lake, continued on around the north shore, and then turned south down the east side of it, going past several Indian villages on or near the shore. He finally reached Kern and Buena Vista Lakes in the most southern part of the valley. From Buena Vista, he rode north and then east across a wide and shallow slough to the eastern foothills and then turned north. He kept to the foothills, crossing the Kaweah, the Kings and the San Joaquin rivers.

When he reached the latter, he turned west, following that river until he found the place where water from Tulare Lake would sometimes gently pour north into the San Joaquin, using a little catchment or lake called Summit Lake. It was high water that season, and a little leaf dropped from a sycamore tree along the way was carried busily along, traveling north to join its brethren in the San Joaquin River, later to be jostled into San Francisco Bay.

Derby then went a little southwest to Tulare Lake and out of the valley by way of Avenal Creek on the west side and returned to San Miguel Mission.

His report of the journey was not too optimistic. Much of the land he traversed he claimed to be spongy and "leached out" because it was constantly subjected to standing water, and then dried out and baked in the sun.

But. . .Captain Derby had found the outlet of Tulare Lake.

Bishop Kipp

At dawn, a steamer glided in and anchored opposite San Pedro, near the Spanish village of Los Angeles on an early morning in 1855. Two passengers, a tall man in black cape and hat and a young fellow also dressed in black, came ashore from one of the small boats sent out to the ship. From somewhere a wagon was produced, carrying a small band of soldiers from Fort Tejon (an outpost in the mountains to the north).

The man was Bishop Kipp and the young man, about 14 years of age, was his son. Kipp had been sent out from the Episcopal House of Bishops in Albany, New York, to be Missionary Bishop of all of California. This was his first visit to his San Joaquin Valley territory. There was an overnight stop at San Fernando Mission and a long trip up San Francisquito Creek to two lakes in the mountains, then down to the Fort which was situated in a small, oak-forested valley, prelude to the long, extensive valley beyond.

He and his son traveled by wagon and at times by horseback. At the settlements they visited, the bishop held church services, baptized children and performed marriages. The two stayed at Fort Tejon for several days.

The Bishop's next stop was at the Sebastian Indian Reservation 15 miles east of Fort Tejon. He saw a thousand Indians gathered for a mourning dance and ceremony. He saw them with feather headdresses, necklaces of bear claws, and painted bodies, gleaming in the firelight, chanting and singing endlessly to the accompaniment of clap-sticks. He heard the chiefs declaim the prowess of those of their tribe who had died and saw them dramatize the events that ended in death.

The pious churchman was overcome with the strangeness of these other-culture people, and put the question in his diary, "Can anything be done for their spiritual benefit?" Then, leaving the reservation the next day, still troubled by the enormous gulf between the two cultures, he wrote, "No man cared for their souls."[1]

Pains In All Their Bones

A pioneer who wished to make a survey of possible farm sites with the idea of getting a grant, attached himself to a trapping party that went north through the valley in 1832. He wished to remain anonymous, but when the group pressed him for a name, he said he could be called Mr. Trapper. He was amazed at the great number of Indians in the valley; there were thousands of them. He reported that he saw the shores of rivers and lakes studded with Indian villages with fifty to a hundred huts in every village. But a great scourge attacked these people. It was probably a particularly strong form of malaria which gave people pains in all their bones, fever, and a terrible headache. There was a general coldness and stiffness of the limbs and body, with violent shaking. It was especially deadly for the Indians who had no immunity for the white man's diseases. (They were not aware that the infection was carried by a mosquito.)

On his return south through the valley in 1833, Mr. Trapper found the Indian population decimated. At first, those dying had been buried by those not affected by the disease. Those lucky enough to have relatives in the foothills retreated there if they could.

---

[1] Right Reverend Wm. S. Kipp; *Early days of my Episcopate: the Journey of Rev. Kipp Through the Valley, 1855.*

Of those remaining, so many died that they resorted to cremating the bodies; and, at last, there was no one left to take care of the dead. They were left in their huts and among the trees, unattended and rotting.

Of course those who had fled to the mountains returned after the cold weather set in and had the task of burying the dead and bringing things back to normal. Whole villages had been wiped out; whole tribes had disappeared.

Had this pestilence not occurred, the flood of gold-seekers which swept across the northern part of the San Joaquin Valley in 1849 and 1850 would have met with much more resistance on the part of the natives. History would have been different.

In the light of later research,[1] it is estimated that 75% of the native population died in 1833. Mr. Trapper, whose real purpose was to find land for himself, and whose report in the press gave us this information about the situation in the valley in 1833, continued on to Southern California and eventually settled there.

---

[1] Sherburne Friend Cook, "The Epidemic of 1830-1833 in California and Oregon," *Publications in American Archaeology and Ethnol-ogy*, Berkeley: University of California Press, Vol. 43, No. 3, 1955.

CHAPTER VI

HISTORY

THE IMPERIAL MAMMOTH AND THE AMERICAN MASTODON

Megafauna

Long, long ago the valley was here, but it did not look as it does today. The silt carried down from the mountains has since "filled in" the valley and more or less leveled it. People have found huge animal bones deep in the silt and clay-- 25 feet deep --in the middle of what is now a dry lake. The bones were those of the mammoth and the mastodon, which roamed wooded valleys all over the world. They were once here in our valley; now they are extinct.

There were other animals here. In the tar pit at the south end of the valley near the town of Maricopa, there are bones of other animals (the sabre tooth tiger, the short faced bear, the jaguar, the great ground sloth, teratornis), bones of animals that are also found in the tar pits at La Brea in Los Angeles County. Those were sucked down by an oil ooze, bubbling, unsolid, the animals caught in it dragged down intact, all in one piece; but at the "dig" at the Maricopa pit in this valley the oil was less runny, more like an asphalt ooze. The bones were all broken up in splinters, in pieces jumbled in a heap, just like in the game of Jack Straws. They were blackened and not fossilized. But they were there --in fact, still are.

Several men took part in the "dig" at Maricopa in the 1950s. They came up from the Los Angeles Museum of Natural History funded by a patron of that museum. But the "dig" had its drawbacks. Four of the men were stricken with valley fever, and two were hospitalized. The germs were in the old dust and soil where they worked. So the dig was abandoned. The oil company which owned the land dumped several tons of sand on the dig and filled it in.

We know now that the larger mammals were here in this valley as early as twelve thousand years ago, and probably much more. Scientists think that people followed the animals. They were hunters.

When ice covered the earth during the ice age, the water of the planet was taken up in ice; the land stuck farther out of the water. The coast line of North America was 600 feet lower than it is now.

Scientists think people from Northern Siberia or North China followed the animals.

In Alaska there seemingly was a "corridor", a green valley surfaced with lakes, between mountains of ice extending from the north latitudes of Alaska down through the great basin, to warmer climates. It led to Lake Mojave to what is now known as the Colorado desert and lower California.

Ancient Tulare Lake

Through this corridor, perhaps as long as 10,000 years ago, there were visitors to Tulare Lake. Perhaps they stayed only during summers when large animals sought water at the lake, or during the spring and fall when migratory birds followed their annual fly-way. Maybe sometimes they "wintered over," told their stories around campfires, decorated themselves with strings of beads made of steatite, or fashioned tools and arrow points. (Scientists think they were not Yokuts or Hokans, but people who preceded the Yokuts). They were wanderers, migrants, strong, weathered, tough-fibred men, women, and children, probably traveling in bands or in families.

Much more than that we do not know at present, but one thing is notable: they made Clovis points and Atlatl.[1] Both of these were important improvements in weapons used to kill large animals, the megafauna. The Clovis points were fairly large, thin points with long, smooth flake scars. One or more short flakes were removed from the base towards the middle of the point. These flake scars give a channeling or "fluting" character to the point. That made it easier for the point to be tightly fastened to a spearshaft. It was a step toward an improvement of an important tool for hunting the large animals which existed then.

---

[1] A carbon 14 test dated these arrow points at 12,000 years ago.

The Atlatl was also an improvement on a lance or spear. It had the effect of lengthening the distance from hunter to animal and with a mightier thrust, the hunter could wound the animal with less danger to himself.

Other Clovis points and Clovis-like points have been found in other places in Indian country. The first find was in a site near Clovis, New Mexico (hence the name) where a point was discovered in close contact with mammoth bones. Then 4,000 to 6,000 years ago there was a great change in the environment which favored more plant life.

To measure this climate change, scientists took samples of soil, tested to be before that date, and counted the grains of pollen in a cubic centimeter. They found 200 grains to the cubic centimeter. When they tested soil dated after 10,000 years ago, they counted the pollen grains and found 2,000 in a cubic centimeter, a dramatic change! There was a tremendous increase in flowering plants and trees. As the effects of this wonderful change were felt, the bounty of nature multiplied and advanced up the food chain, animals and humans increasing greatly.

The people who ventured into the New World brought their culture with them, primitive though it probably was. There was certainly language. They would need it to communicate if they were to have success in hunting the larger animals. They may have had little time to develop the arts, but probably there were stories, myths, and tales told around the campfires at night. They must have also brought with them their religion, their shaman, and their songs.

The Discovery of the San Joaquin Valley

After the first missions were well established, soldiers and priests were sent on expeditions to explore the land and convert the Indians. Such a pair were Captain Pedro Fages (Fa'hes) of the Spanish Cavalry, and Fray (Fry) Juan Crespi. Their discoveries were in two scenes:

Scene I: In the Spring of 1772, The Expedition of Fages and Crespi

The purpose of this expedition was to find a way to Point Reyes, across the bay and about 30 miles north of San Francisco. The currents and crosscurrents in what is now called the Golden Gate were too dangerous to take a force of soldiers across the waters in small boats. The expedition's story is from Crespi's diary:

"We were surprised that the Bay of San Francisco extended so far inland, and as the magnitude of the expedition began to show itself, we climbed the northeast shoulder of Mount Diablo to get a larger view. We saw before us a great plain running northeast to southwest, as level as the palm of the hand," wrote Fray Crespi.

He went on to explain that the estuary they had been following was fed by two large rivers, one from the north (the Sacramento) and one from the south (the San Joaquin), and the one from the south was fed by two large rivers, before joining with the one from the north. He wrote that where the two large rivers combined, there was a large island--and so it is today, well almost--instead of one large island, there are several close together.

It was a magnificent view; it was a grand and plenteous effluence of water. The natives brought presents of seeds, *"a bow trimmed with feathers, the pelt of an animal, and arrows which they had thrust into the ground"*. The Spanish responded with beads and strings of beads.

They would need boats to get across the several large rivers and find their way to Point Reyes; or if they went south and explored the valley and attempted to cross the rivers there, they would need a larger force and more provisions, so they decided to return to Monterey.

On the hill above the place where fresh river water and salt ocean water met (Antioch), Fages and Crespi had a long talk with their Indian guides. The latter told of the great extent of the valley, how it reached a village in the south called Buena Vista or "Good View," and how that village was on an elevation near a large lake by the same name.

They described the clothes the Indians wore, how they made their huts out of tules and their use of tobacco as food and all the features of their material culture. Fages took notes of everything that they discussed so that he could later make a report to the Viscount back in Spain. It was fortunate that he had this opportunity to learn of the culture as it was before any change had been made. Fages realized some of the great possibilities of this new land.

On their return to Monterey, Fages was promoted to head commander of military forces in California and transferred to San Diego. There he watched for an opportunity to see for himself the southern part of the San Joaquin Valley.

Scene II: In the Fall of 1772

Captain Fages and his contingent of soldiers and guides had trailed three Spanish deserters for days and even weeks from Mission San Diego. From San Diego they had gone east to Imperial Valley, over the mountains, and then northeast to San Bernardino Valley, then through Cajon Pass, along the edge of the Mojave Desert, through Antelope Valley, Borrego Valley, and Coyote Canyon to the San Jacinto mountains, then northwest across to Tejon pass. They viewed the beautiful little oak-covered valley whose eye was blue, Lake Castaic, edged in white salt, an entry-way to the pass that descended into the vast San Joaquin valley below. We can imagine the following scene unfolding.

The captain held his breath as he surveyed a scene so vast as to be almost unbelievable. Who would have suspected that behind the facade of the Coast Range, a familiar view from the missions on the coast, would be this huge valley with lakes, swamps and groves of trees in a seemingly endless plain? He had taken a detour and ascended the hill which guarded the steep pass (the grapevine), that descended into the valley, in order to get a view from a greater height. Ducks and geese circled around the vast marsh area, a wintering ground for seemingly millions of birds. The flapping and whirring of wings and the calls of birds filled the air. This was a great fly-way and the marsh was a nesting habitat for birds coming from the north to the warmer climate of California.

From his view at the top of the pass he could see a lake (Kern Lake) sparkling at the foot of the hill, and another larger one (Lake Buena Vista), nestled in the brown hills at his left. Overlooking the shores of the lake was an Indian village of tule huts (Tulumneu). Glimpses of water surrounded by tules, and occasionlly shaded by willows, defined waterways that he thought must emanate from the hills and mountains to his distant right. The blue far-away mountains to his left, he probably thought of as the Coast Range, but he would learn on his return to the Mission San Luis Obispo that it was another range, the Diablo Range, that paralleled the Coast Range.

Tucked away at the foot of the pass which he and his followers would soon descend, was another Indian village. Grapevines grew in this sheltered place and the Indians trained them to climb on trees

and bushes so that they would produce grapes. The place was called "the grapevine." There was no reference to this village in his notes, but we may assume that Fages sent his Indian guides to give his greetings before continuing on his way.

Fages had been very well educated in Spain, and he seemed to have a penchant for exploration. He had joined the expedition of Portola' which went north from Monterey and made the discovery of San Francisco Bay. Small wonder then, that he had been interested in exploring the eastern reaches of San Franciso bay that spring. He and Crespi had discovered the northern reaches of the great San Joaquin Valley!

Both he and Crespi kept diaries of that trip. Crespi's has already been quoted here. Fages' diary[1], with the addenda, was found by scholars later. It had a "Nota" added to it describing the San Joaquin Valley as far south as Buena Vista Lake and village and the plain that continues past them for seven leagues until one goes up a steep incline where grew many grapevines and through a small valley to the south, thickly grown with groves of live oaks.

But Fages did not mention Tulare Lake in his report because he, himself, had not seen it. His supplies were low, and the men and guides were fatigued with their long journey. Their summer uniforms, suitable for the climate of San Diego, would not be warm enough for the valley fog in the fall of the year. He realized that it was of no use to look any longer for the three deserters as they could easily lose themselves in the vast valley he had now discovered.

---

[1] Pedro Fages, *A Historical, Political and Natural Description of California*, newly translated into English from the original Spanish by Herbert Ingram Priestley. Berkeley: University of California Press, 1937.

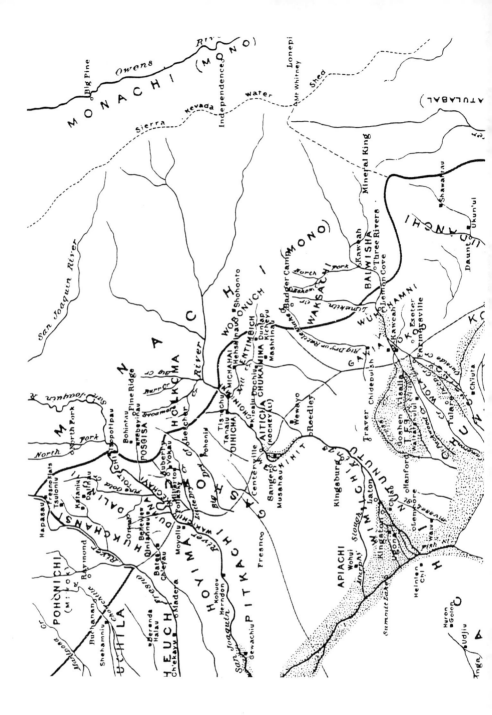

130

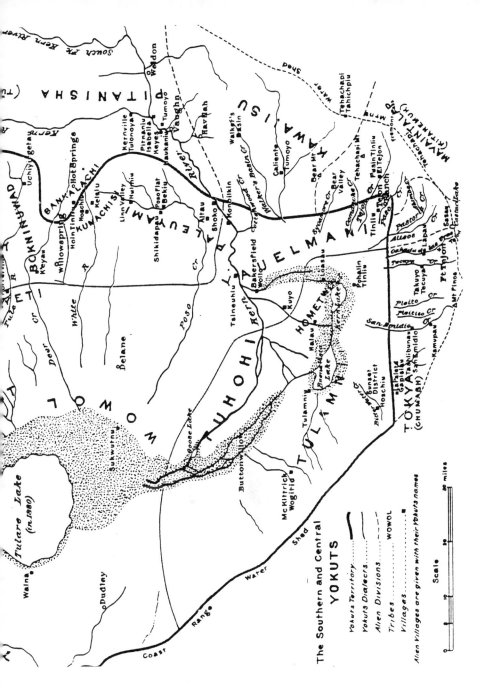

Indian villages of the southern San Joaquin Valley were plotted in A. L. Kroeber's Handbook of the Indians of California, 1925, Bulletin 78 of the Bureau of American Ethnology of the Smithsonian Institution.

131

The party rode down the steep slopes of Grapevine Canyon, explored Wheeler Ridge and turned north through El Paso de la Plieta from which they had another splendid view of the San Joaquin Valley, as it was later named.

Then they traveled to the west side of Buena Vista Lake to the village of Tulumneu.[1] From there Fages and his mounted troops made their way to Mission San Luis Obispo near the coast.

The discovery of the fabulous San Joaquin Valley was all in 1772. But Fages' report to the Vicount in Spain was not written until 1775. Why the delay? Could it be that the expedition encountered inclement weather when it reached the southern entrance to the valley? Perhaps the dramatic scene where Fages ascended the hill and viewed the valley to infinity was pure fiction. Instead, they may have encountered the mist and fog left over from a recent rain as is so often experienced in the valley in the fall of the year when no following storm and wind is engendered to lift the remnants of the preceding rain over the barrier of the mountains. The rain-soaked soil would give up its moisture to the air above in the form of fog. That fog would cling lovingly to the familiar scene, reducing visibility on the ground to half-a-mile or less. Loath to depart, the fog would wait for another storm with wind and rain to clear the air..

Fages would not wish to report the unfavorable weather, yet he could not write of the south end of the valley with only the testimony of Indian guides. He must wait until some qualified white traveler would confirm the temporary condition.

---

[1] Fages could not then have known that one of the runaways he had been following would come to that village later and take an Indian wife. A descendant of that union is living now (1992) at the Tule River Reservation near Porterville.

José Antonio Carrillo

José Antonio Carrillo was a son of Raymundo, who was clerk and administrator of Santa Barbara Mission and thereafter filled several civil and political offices. José Antonio had three brothers, and the four of them were all large, handsome men over six feet tall. It was jokingly said that the sum of their weights would have been a thousand pounds, or half a ton. José Antonio had military training in Mexico where he attained the rank of Lieutenant Colonel. He was a charming and persuasive man, strongly desireous of maintaining his status in the Mexican regime but almost always finding himself on the losing side. He signed the treaty of Cahuenga as the Mexican Commissioner in 1847 where John Charles Fremont signed for the Americans. In 1849, he was a member of the constitutional convention. After that, his public life seemed to be over and he died in 1862 at the age of 66. So say the chronicles of the times.

His name had been constantly before the California public for 25 years. Bancroft says, "No one excelled him in intrigue and he was never without a plot on hand." It was said that there was nothing he would not do to oblige a friend or get the better of a foe. He was a gambler of loose habits and utterly careless in his associations, yet he never lost the privilege of associating with the best people or the power of winning their friendship.

In this author's opinion, José Antonio (Carrillo) was most likely the one who signed his name (José Antonio) on the treaty for the Tachis in 1851. While those two names, José Antonio are as common among Mexicans as John is among English-Americans, the character of José as described by Bancroft, tells of a man who would take great pleasure in negotiating with the Americans a treaty advantageous to the Tachis on all points possible. The Americans had been foes of Carrillo in 1846.

As the Americans were getting ready to establish themselves in the L.A. area, José Antonio Carrillo, who was a one-time mayor of Los Angeles and a judge as well, appeared with 120 well-armed, mounted men. A four-pound swivel gun earlier sequestered by a Mexican woman was brought out. The Americans fell back and in retreat were boarding a ship at San Pedro. But then, Fremont appeared with his considerable force of 150 mounted riflemen, and eventually the "Californians" (Mexicans), hindered by dissensions, poor powder, and lack of leadership, ended the revolt. Both José Antonio Carrillo and John Charles Fremont signed the Cahuenga treaty on January 13, 1847.

In 1849, the Californians participated in the making of a state constitution. Among them was José Antonio Carrillo because he was an important man and would be able to give the important viewpoints of those who formerly ruled the land. After that, Carrillo seems to have disappeared from public life and it was not until notice of his death in 1862 that he again comes to our attention. However, the following is a tale that needs telling, not only because it may have some connection with the Tachi-Yokuts tribe in their troubled times, but also because it shows activities and general attitudes of Indian during 1843 to the 1856 period.

A grant called El Tejon was given by Governor Micheltorena to two men; Spanish-born Jose Antonio Aquirre, and a native of Mexico named del Valle. Both were residents of Los Angeles at the time the grant was received. They requested Don Joaquin (a pseudonym?) Carrillo, alcalde and judge of the First Instance at Los Angeles, to go to the ranch and, according to the custom of the times, give them judicial possession. He refused because of fear of the Indians. But "in 1850 Carrillo took 600 cows to the Tulare Lake region for summer grazing."[1]

---

[1] Wallace Smith, *Garden of the Sun*, 1939, 4th ed., reprint, Fresno: Hardison-A-1 Printers, 1960.

Whether it was Carrillo or someone else, someone came to the aid of the Tachis in negotiating the treaty, and when the treaties were not ratified by the Senate, someone advised them to rebel at a more opportune time. Someone planned their fortifications at Battle Mountain in 1856 and Gregorio was there to build them.

Someone sent word down to the Tachi tribelet that the State treasury was bare and neither the State Militia nor the federal troops had been paid for several months and that they would probably cast a cold eye on any orders to go to the defense of settlers in a distant Indian uprising. In San Francisco there were fires doing millions of dollars worth of damages and a second vigilantia had been organized.

This was the opportunity Quintin and the Tachis had been waiting for. Gregorio and some of the Tachis went across the valley and, near the Tule River on a hill selected by Carrillo, they built a stone wall and fort.

John Charles Fremont

A great need was felt for more accurate knowledge of the vast wilderness between the frontier of the United States and the Pacific Coast. People wondered. . . What was out there?. . .and how troublesome were the Indians? John Charles Fremont, a lieutenant in the Bureau of Topographical Engineers, was chosen to organize and carry on an expedition financed by the U.S. Government. He was young, but had experience under capable leadership in exploring the wilderness to the north. He was to make observations of all sorts in preparation for map-making--to observe plants, grasses, trees, the nature of the soil, availability of water, the animals, the Indians, and many other features likely to be of interest to those who looked toward the west.

In all, he made five expeditions between the dates of 1842 and 1854. When each one was completed, he wrote a report with the aid of his wife Jessie (a beautiful young woman), the daughter of prominent Senator Benton. No doubt her talents as a writer contributed to the success of the reports. These reports read like a James Fennimore Cooper novel. The Fremonts were a handsome couple and became America's sweethearts. It was in the second expedition that events occurred of interest to us.

His first expedition went no farther west than the South Pass and the Rockies. They then stopped at Sutter's Fort and about a month later, they went through the San Joaquin Valley to the Tehachapis and on back to the States. Through these expeditions, he showed how it would be possible for parties to cross the territory between the east and the west and finally arrive in California.

The second expedition started in St. Louis, went northwesterly to Oregon, the Dalles, then went south near the eastern side of the Cascade Range. It crossed the Sierra Nevada by way of Carson City and continued until it reached Sacramento. There, they recuperated a month with Captain J.A. Sutter and then went south through the San Joaquin Valley (more of this later) through Walker pass in the Tehachapis, northeast across the Mohave desert and terminated at Kansas City. Somewhere during the course of the trip, two California Indian "boys" were added. Their names were Juan and Gregorio. They were not really "boys". Gregorio, for instance, had been baptised at Santa Inez Mission in 1804 at the age of three. This author believes that this was the same Gregorio who was identified with the Tachis at the signing of the treaty in 1851.

On his second expedition Fremont wrote a description of the San Joaquin Valley as he traversed it north to south. It was springtime in the month of April in 1844. His horse tread noiselessly over a thick, green carpet of alfrilaria and soft, pink, owl's clover. Blue lupines bloomed amidst a sea of golden poppies.

"One might travel the whole world over," he wrote, "without finding a valley more fresh and verdant --more bounteously watered than in the San Joaquin Valley."[1]

136

History and Politics

Nearly 80 years after the discovery of the San Joaquin Valley, a traveler and his Indian guide came north from Los Angeles by way of Grapevine Pass. The white man was a reporter who planned to write an article about his travels through the San Joaquin, especially the southern part. It was to be titled, "The Tulare Lakes". The year was 1851.

He saw first the smaller Kern Lake which emptied westerly into Lake Buena Vista, a larger one, and he observed the swampy slough country as water sluggishly flowed north from there to the much larger Tulare Lake. He wrote: "at the point where the slough issues from the lower lake {and enters Tulare Lake} the sheet of water is so broad (30 or 40 miles) that no boundary can be discerned on the other side, save the purple streak which marks the Sierra Nevada."

The reporter traveled farther north and encountered a large Indian village on the north shore of Tulare Lake. Again he wrote:

> At this point reside the Attache {Tachi-Yokuts} nation of Indians, or that portion of them governed by Tinsin, one of the most powerful braves in the southern section of the country.
> The Rancheria is a large one, consisting of some very large huts, built entirely of tules, and capable each of accommodating from 10 to 15 persons. Tinsin himself, a brawny giant whose frame would compare advantageously with that of any Mountain Chief and who boasts of five wives, possessed a hut in which twenty men could easily sleep. The rancheria is built on the border of the lake, and not a tree is to be seen within miles of it.[1]

---

[1] From *A Collection of Ethnographical Articles On The California Indians*, edited by Robert F. Heizer, Ramona, CA: Ballena Press Publications in Archaeology, Ethnology and History, No. 7, 1976 #15, *The Tulare Lakes*, Anonymous. From the San Francisco Picayune, November 15, 1851.

Who was this Tinsin? "A brawny giant" is not the usual description of a Yokuts chief. The Yokuts are usually of average height or less and of stocky build, even described sometimes as barrel-chested. Often they could be called spare, not heavily muscled, but strong nevertheless. Could the name have been mistakenly heard by the traveling reporter? Could the name have been - - Quintin?

Quintin was the name signed to Treaty A which was negotiated between the Tachis and the U.S. Commissioners in 1851.

Both names, Tinsin and Quintin, are not at all like other Yokuts names. Quintin was the name of an Indian who was associated with an Indian chief named Marin who, with a force of Indian tribes in the vicinity of San Rafael (on San Francisco Bay), rebelled in 1824 against the Mexican troops there.

Marin was captured and sent to prison, but Quintin sought refuge in a point of land since known as Punta de Quintin. He was a daring warrior and quite young. When he was captured on the point, he was taken to San Francisco where he was placed in the custody of the priests at Mission Dolores. He was detained at the mission for two years and at the end of that time he was set at liberty, there being no doubt that the whites could rely on his promises.

> *"Quintin was a good sailor," wrote General Vallejo. During his detention he was employed by the missionary Fathers as skipper of one of the lighters trading the bay. Fifteen years later at the recommendation of the military officers who had given me their guarantee of his good behavior, I placed him in charge of my best lighter which was engaged in making trips between Sonoma Creek and Yerba Buena,[1] (San Francisco).*

The spot where Quintin was captured became known as Punta de Quintin. When the Americans arrived, they changed the name

---

[1] Mariano Gualdalupe Vallejo, "*Report on History of Marin County*," Marin Co. Library, 1880.

of that place to Punta de San Quentin, believing that adding San (Saint) before names of the towns or villages that they visited would gain for them the good will of the Catholics and so when they built a prison at that point, the name became known throughout California as San Quentin Prison.

We can speculate that as time went on Quintin began to long for the wild country and the freedom he had experienced in his youth. By 1846, when Mexico was defeated by the Americans, the terms of the treaty gave the Territory of California to the United States. It might have been that at this time Quintin sought out the Tachis. Being a born leader, and a partially educated man, it was not strange that the Tachis made him their chief. It was not strange either that other Indian leaders would be attracted to this tribe which was living healthily and enthusiastically in a protected environment that furnished them plenteously with food.

What glorious summers, full of ceremonies, gatherings with other tribelets, feastings, songs, dancing, and games the Yokuts must have had in those few years around 1846. Leaders from the outside brought new life and confidence to the tribe. What full winters there were! Myths, stories, and old traditions were remembered and taught to the young, and the old were revered for their wisdom.

And the young men, fired with confidence given them by this new leader (or leaders), took their arrow-making more seriously. They fashioned their bows, practiced archery, and went on hunting expeditions.

[1] Wallace Smith, *Garden of the Sun*, 4th edition, Fresno: Hardison A-1 Printers, 1960, p 72.

It was virgin land. No plow had touched it, as yet. It was not pollution which clouded the view of the mountains from the green plains below. But the foothills were veiled and obscured by the morning mists until, gradually by mid-morning, the sun vanquished them.

The Governor of California from 1836 to 1842 was Juan Bautista Alvarado. He sent Don Santiago Estrada into the valley in command of troops with orders to subdue the Indians along the foothills to the east. After his term of office had expired, Alvarado secured a grant of land in those foothills which ran from Mariposa south to the point where the San Joaquin River comes from the mountains to the plains. Later, he sold this land, which was named "Las Mariposas," to John C. Fremont. It is hard to believe that these orders by Alvarado were the only ones of that kind issued by him to Estrada or to any state commander for a like purpose. Indians were sporadically stealing horses from the coast regions or falling upon isolated settlements and much pressure was applied to Alvarado to remedy the situation.

There had never been a treaty between the Indians and the Mexican government, or any government.

And then, events exploded near Sacramento like a bomb that changed night into day.

The Discovery of Gold

Gold had been discovered in 1848! At first people did not hear of it or did not believe it. But by 1849 the gold rush was under way. The northern part of the valley, the Sierra foothills, and Northern California were suddenly overrun by gold seekers, killing or dispersing whole tribes, and dispossessing other tribes of their hunting and food-gathering lands. Some of the newcomers believed that the Indians should be made to give way before the advancing tide of white settlers. There were expeditions of extermination and agreements for Indian removal. Stealing horses and foodstuffs by Indians was followed by wars against them everywhere. The northern valley Yokuts were destroyed, and farms and settlements of white people took their places.

In 1850 the Yokuts in the southern part of the valley began to be invaded by the sobered miners intent on finding a farm for themselves and their families. On September 9, 1850, California became a state of the Union!

In December of that year, John Woods with a party of 15 men came down from Sacramento with a herd of cattle and built a cabin on a creek, about 5 miles east of present Visalia.

The Indians watched and waited. They saw cattle grazing on the nearby hills where deer sometimes passed. They saw the cabin near the wild blackberry vines that had always furnished them with berries, and they saw the oak trees cut down to make the cabin. This was a sizable group of men. It was best to stop in the beginning any plans they might have for the future.

Accordingly, the chief and a few Indians appeared at the cabin and requested John Woods to leave. They would expect him and his men to be gone in 10 days.

The rest of the story is well-known. The white men buried their plow and other equipment, but for some reason, they were delayed in getting their cattle off the hills within the 10 days limit. All but two of the men were killed by the Indians and a patch of skin from John Woods' body was nailed to a tree. A gruesome story! Two crawled away in the underbrush and told the frightening tale to a settler in the vicinity.

The matter was taken up with the chief, Francisco, by some of the settlers later. He brought two of his tribe who were already in disgrace and they were tried, found guilty and sentenced to death. One tried to escape and was shot, the other faked death and later escaped.

Treaties With the Indians

The next year, 1851, when the roving reporter first saw the Tachi-Yokuts village at the head of Tulare Lake, three men appointed by the United States Government came into the valley to talk with the Indian tribes. They came with three, six-mule team covered wagons, 150 pack animals, 100 soldiers, and ten officers. The three commissioners made the first treaty with the Chowchillas, and it was called Treaty "N". After that, they divided their equipment, supplies, and men equally between them, and each commissioner took a certain section of the state to negotiate with their separate tribes or groups of tribes.

The treaty negotiated with the Tachis and nine other Yokuts tribelets was called Treaty "A". The idea in the minds of the commissioners was to give the Indians land in the plains area, thus leaving the foothills for the miners. The treaty gave them a long, narrow strip of land six miles wide on the plains, extending from the Chowchilla River on the north to the Kaweah River on the south. The lower border would follow the Kaweah River and Cross Creek in a northwestern direction until it reached Tulare lake, then would proceed in a northwesterly direction along the lake shore to the mouth of the Kings River. It would continue north and northeast on that river until it reached a point six miles west of the boundary of Treaty "N". By these terms, the Tachis were cleverly able to retain the site of their village of Waiu. Who would have been able to maneuver such terms? Who signed the treaty for the Tachis?

It was signed by five Indians:
Quintin
Jose Antonio
Sulio
Elario
Gregorio

By their names we may infer that they had all been at the missions, had learned to speak Spanish, and had acquired some education. Nevertheless, they all signed with a mark. Had they come into this sparsely settled area to make a last-ditch effort to save some territory for the Indians, for Indians only?

We know now who Quintin was. He was undoubtedly the Indian who had been a rebel in his early youth and who had been put under the guardianship of the priests at Dolores Mission at Yerba Buena in lieu of prison. He was taught how to sail the lighter across the bay from Sonoma to Yerba Buena to bring fresh produce for the mission kitchen. Later, when he was freed from detention by the Fathers, he was engaged by General Vallejo to ply the waters in that gentlemen's service in his best lighter.

And who was Gregorio? He was born at Santa Inez Mission in 1801 and baptized in 1804. It is doubtful that he was Yokuts, but he supposedly had the blood of chiefs in his veins. He joined Fremont's expedition as the latter passed through the valley in 1844 and spent the following winter in Kentucky where he had charge of Fremont's prize horses. Later he returned to California and was a member of Fremont's famed battalion during the Mexican War in 1846.

Gregorio again journeyed east with Fremont and was a member of Fremont's disastrous expedition of 1848 when many of the party died. Gregorio distinguished himself many times on this trip by his bravery and fortitude.

At times during those years Gregorio lived with the Fremonts as a servant. But on New Year's night, 1850, the Fremont family boarded a ship at Monterey, bound for New York. Gregorio came to see them off and to bring a going-away gift of some moccasins to Lily, their young daughter. He wept at their departure. John Charles Fremont had been elected Senator from California! The Fremonts were to live in Washington D.C. Gregorio was on his own. Apparently it was at this time he joined the Tachis by the great Tulare Lake.

On the books at Mission Santa Inez Gregorio was listed as a stonemason. We think he was to use this skill for the benefit of the Tachis in a very few years.

Politics and Military Maneuvers

On July 7, 1846, the U.S. flag was raised at Monterey and subsequently at Yerba Buena, Sonoma, Bodega Bay, and Sutters Fort. There was no Mexican flag to be hauled down and had not been for two months as Mexico was at war with the United States and Mexico could no longer sustain its hold over ports in northern California.

Afterwards, forces of horsemen were sent south headed by Fremont,[1] Beale, and Mervine to take Los Angeles and San Diego from the Mexicans. At first, there was no resistance at Los Angeles. But there soon appeared a party of 120 well-armed, mounted Mexicans under Captain Jose` Antonio Carrillo, which took the village out of the hands of the Americans. Soon, however, news came of the defeat of the Mexican army in New Mexico and Texas. The Mexican troops were left stranded without supplies. They may have disbanded, each allowed to find his way back to Mexico as best he could. Did the Mexican captain and some of his followers go north into the San Joaquin Valley then? They had a common enemy--the Americans!

---

[1] Fremont was a spare, active man about 33. When he went south in '46, after the flag was raised at Monterey, he had about 150 men called the "Native Battalion of Mounted California Volunteer Riflemen." It consisted of a bodyguard of five Delaware Indians: Lt. Gillesby; scouts Kit Carson, Joseph Walker, and Alex Godey, Gregorio; trappers from the interior wilds; Indians, voyageurs, and settlers.

Things were in a state of confusion and uncertainty in 1846. California was now a territory of the United States by terms of the treaty with Mexico. Did that include the Central Valley?

It did include the Central Valley. The discovery of gold in the mountains near Sacramento was yet to occur, the consequent rush to the gold fields of 80,000 people in 1850 sounded the death knell for these Yokuts who lived in their way. They fled or were killed by the oncoming hordes of would-be miners. When Alfred Louis Kroeber came into the valley from the University of California at Berkeley, he did not try to find any Indians in the Central Valley north of the Fresno River.

The Tule River War - 1856

Discord between Indians and whites was nothing new in the area of the Tulare Lake basin. Just six years earlier, in December of 1850, the John Woods party of fifteen men and a herd of cattle came down from Sacramento in December. They built a cabin and put their cattle out to graze on the small hills to the east. They were later massacred by the Indians for overstaying the 10-day time limit set by the Indians. Forays against each other occurred now and then for the next several years.

Cooler heads did what they could. Indians camped close to Visalia were brought into town for their own protection. Others became rightfully alarmed at the talk of the white men. Indians, from the Kaweah River to Fort Tejon, began to congregate at the Tule River, probably for their own protection.

This further alarmed settlers, and finally Judge John Cutler authorized a company of mounted riflemen to be paid by the State. Fifty-six men signed up on March 29 and elected Foster DeMasters their captain. They signed up but were never paid as there was no money in the State treasury.

At length DeMasters' men rode to the Tule River to check on reports of gathering Indians. An independent group of nine men rode further to Tailholt and attacked a group of Tejon Indians, killing five. Some said the Indians were bent on a massacre of whites living along the White River. (Later, this was doubted as the Indians had women and children with them.)

DeMasters followed up the Tule River several miles and spotted smoke from the Indians' campfires. They discovered the well-protected site the Indians now occupied. The attack was made without hesitation, but a shower of arrows from the breastworks drove them back. They retreated to a mile away and awaited reinforcement. When settlers arrived from the south, their number was about 140.

Another assault was made and it too was repulsed. Small skirmishes continued over the next few days until 25 soldiers and a howitzer arrived from Fort Miller (near Fresno) and more mounted cavalry came from Fort Tejon. The attacking force now numbered about 400 and the Indians around 700. The hostilities had been underway for nearly a month. A plan was laid to attack at daybreak the following day.

The Tachis had practiced diligently and were quite accurate with their bows and arrows but from such a distance they were largely ineffectual. The arrows were striking the enemies' jackets and were getting caught in the material, but were unable to pierce it. The Tachis evidently had no idea that the cannon had arrived and was available to be used against them.

The settlers and the troops wrestled the small cannon with the aid of horses on a hill opposite and a little higher than the hill the Yokuts were defending. But while Captain Livingston from Fort Miller--now in charge--and 60 troops were putting the howitzer in place, the Indians began an offensive of their own. When the Indians saw the cannon being put into place, they made a last desperate attack. The soldiers fired the cannon and the charge landed inside the breastworks of the Indians. They were repulsed in the face of both gunfire and the deadly fire of the cannon.

Livingston then ordered a general charge and the Indians were routed. Most fled into the high country where they had left their women and children.

Over the long campaign no whites were killed but a few were wounded, some seriously. Up to 40 Indians may have been killed, but an accurate count was impossible since the dead and wounded were regularly removed from the scene. The 1856 Tule River Indian War was over. Few were captured in the ensuing chase and the whites, for a time, suffered from the slaughter of cattle and the burning of cabins, 12 houses in all.

One result of the "war" was the forcing of still more Indians into the Kings River and Tule River Indian Farms. These were reservations where the natives were farther yet from their natural grounds and where starvation was a constant companion.

* * * * * * * * * *

HOW COYOTE STOLE THE SUN

CHAPTER VII

THE CONCLUSION

HOW COYOTE STOLE THE SUN

THE CONCLUSION

"And you, Day.
And you, Night.
All of you see me.
One, with this world!"
           - - - from a Yokuts Prayer

What can we ultimately say about the Yokuts tribe? Where do they fit in the greater scheme of all California American Indian history and culture? What information we have on the tribe specifically, we owe mostly to the careful notations of J.P. Harrington and A.L. Kroeber, whose early twentieth century explorations of Central California Indian life, form the basis of most tribal studies today.

The rest, we must glean from the bits and pieces of the many scattered sources that lie, frequently untouched, on library and museum shelves; that lurk in collections of notes from explorers, adventurers, historians, and linguists; that are found in the evidence of archaeologists and their digs; and that are preserved in the diaries and correspondence of the occasional observant reporter and traveler. The task of reconstructing California's Native American past, and giving it its proper place and meaning, is a truly monumental one, continued each day in the careful and caring research of many a hard-working scholar.

We are able to speak with some degree of certitude, however, about certain aspects of this particular Indian tribe. As has been seen in this present book, today's Tachi-Yokuts, living at the Santa Rosa Rancheria south of Lemoore, going to school, working, leading the lives of the 1990s, have in fact rich traditions that deserve preservation. We know that the ancestors of these Yokuts must have come to the San Joaquin Valley, and to the shores of the great Tulare Lake, many hundreds of years ago---bringing with them the dreams, visions, and lifestyle of a culture at one with nature. Around the campfires there were myths and songs. For these people, each and every ceremony carried a religious and philosophical significance.

Then as the white man and his missions made their impact in the late 1700s and the 1800s, disease struck, the old ways were disrupted, and the records show a culture beginning to crumble. We see the Yokuts succumbing to the great plague of 1833; we read of horse stealing from coastal settlements and the treaty intended to keep the Indians confined to the plains; and finally, we read of the Tule River Indian War--700 Yokuts, facing 400 armed settlers and army troops. We watch the Native American world of the Yokuts fall prey to death, famine, and subjugation---their image as "Digger Indians" labelling them to the white man and to themselves alike, as inferior.

But today, we can take pride in knowing that a much fairer assessment of these native survivors is at last being attempted. We can see that the Yokuts have indeed made an important contribution to California's Native American heritage. For while this tribe may not evidence as vastly recorded an art or dance form as do some others, the great traditions and myths of the Yokuts find able representation in the simple elegance of their woven baskets and in the words and cadence of their many songs and myths. The myths deal with fundamental philosophical problems such as the creation, life and death, good and evil. It has been one of the goals of this book, and of the video which accompanies it, to preserve and pass on these bits of the Yokuts heritage that so richly deserve our appreciation and our attention.

And today, too, this is especially important. For this 1992 book is being published during the 500th anniversary year of Columbus's discovery of the Americas.

CONCLUSION

In 1492 two cultures with fundamentally different world ideas confronted one another: the Greco-Roman, Judeo-Christian, western European world view, and the Native American world view.

They were based on radically different ideas about the nature of the physical world--the former, most often characterized as "scientific," or subject to laws of cause and effect, and the latter, as controlled by the mind in an altered state of consciousness.

At that time, neither culture looked upon the other with any degree of understanding. Now, however, the world is questioning anew the true meaning and impact of this meeting of two different cultures. And it has become time to search out the values and the contribution of the Native American culture to abandon certain outdated attitudes and realize our continuing debt to those who dwelt on this continent for so many years before the white man made his own devastating impact on a rich and thriving native civilization and culture.

* * * * * * * * *

HOW COYOTE STOLE THE SUN

Bibliography

Barker, Captain John, "Indian War in Tulare, *San Joaquin Vignettes: Reminiscences/Captain John Barker*, Seventeenth Annual Publication, Chapt. 3, Kern Co. Historical Society, Bakersfield, Ca., 1955.

Bean, Lowell John, *Mukat's People: The Cahuilla Indians of Southern California*, Berkeley, University of California Press 1972.

Bean, Lowell John, *People of the New World*, Ramona, CA: Ballena Press, 1982.

Bean, Lowell J. and Thomas C. Blackburn, editors, *Native Californians, A Theoretical Retrospective,* Ramona, CA: Ballena Press, 1976.

Blackburn, Thomas C., ""Ceremonial Interaction and Social Interaction in Aboriginal California," ?*ANTAP': California Indian Political and Economnic Organization,* edited by Lowell J. Bean and Thomas F. King, Ramona, CA: Ballena Press, 1974.

Blackburn, Thomas C., *People of the New World*, Ramona, CA: Ballena Press, 1982.

Blackburn, Thomas C., *December's Child: A Book of Chumash Oral Narratives*, Berkeley: University of California Press, 1975.

Bolton, Herbert Eugene, *In the South San Joaquin Ahead of Garces*, Bakersfield, CA: Kern County Historical Society, May 1935.

Boyd, William Harland, *A California Middle Border; the Kern River Country, 1772-1880.* {Richardson, Tx.} Havilah Press, 1972.

Briggs, Carl and Earl Francis Trudell, *Quarterdeck and Saddlehorn, the Story of Edward F. Beal, 1822-1893*, Glendale, CA: A.H. Clark Co., 1983.

Britch, (Devany) Susan, "Tachi: A Systatic Sketch", M.A. Thesis, Californiia State University, Fresno, Ca, 1980, (127 pages).

Brown, James L., *The Story of Kings County California*, Lederer Street and Zeus Co., Inc., Berkeley. In cooperation with the Art Print Shop, Hanford, California, 1941.

Campbell, Joseph, Historical Atlas of World Mythology, Vol. I, "The Way of Animal Powers," Part I. "Mythology of the Primitive Hunters and Gatherers," Part II. "Mythologies of the Great Hunt,". New York: Van der Mark Editions, San Francisco: dist. by Harper & Row, 1988.

Campbell, Joseph, *The Power of Myth*, 1st ed. New York: Bantam, Double Day, Dell Publishing Group Inc., June 1988.

Campbell, Joseph, *Primitive Mythology*, New York: Penguin Books, 1976.

Caughey, John W., California, Englewood Cliffs: Prentice Hall, 1940, 2nd ed., 1953.

Cook, Sherburne Friend, *The Epidemic of 1830-1833 in California and Oregon*, Berkeley & Los Angeles, California: University of California Publications in American Archaeology and Ethnology, Vol. 43, #3, pp. 303-326, 1955.

Cook, S.F., *Colonial Expedition to the Interior of California's Central Valley - 1800-1820*. Berkeley: University of California Press, 1960.

Cook, S. F., *Expedition to the Interior of California, Central Valley, 1820-1840*, Berkeley: University of California Press, 1962.

Costo, Rupert and Jeannette Henry Costo, editors, *The Missions of California, A Legacy of Genocide*, San Francisco: The Indian Historian Press for the American Historical Society, 1987.

Cummins, Marjorie W., *The Tache-Yokuts, Indians of the San Joaquin Valley: Their Lives, Songs and Stories*, Fresno: Pioneer Publishing, 1978, 2nd ed., rev. & enl., 1979.

Davis, Emma Lou, *The Ancient Californians: Rancholabran Hunters of the Mojave Lakes Country*, Los Angeles: Natural History Museum of Los Angeles County, May 1, 1978.

Derby, George H., *The Topographical Reports of Lt. George Derby, 1847*, Francis Forqubar, ed., 1933.

Eldredge, Zoeth Skinner, *History of California, Vol. II*, New York: Century History Company, 1915.

Ellison, Wm. Henry, *The Federal Indian Policy in California, 1846-1860*, Thesis: University of California, San Francisco: R&E Research Associates, reprint, 1974.

Ericson, Jonathon and R.E. Taylor and Rainer Burger, *Peopling the New World*, Los Altos, CA: Ballena Press, 1982.

Fages, Pedro, *A Historical, Political and Natural Description of California*, newly translated into English from the original Spanish by Herbert Ingram Priestley. Berkeley: University of California Press, 1937.

Forbes, Jack D., *Native Americans of California and Nevada*, Healdsburg, CA: Naturegraph Pub., West Laboratory for Education, 1969.

Gayton, Anna H., "Areal Applications of California Folk Tales," AMERICAN ANTHROPOLOGIST, 57: 582-599, 1935.

Gayton, Anna H., "Estudillo Among the Yokuts," Essays in Anthropology presented to A.L. Kroeber, pg. 67-85, Berkeley Press, 1936.

Gayton, Anna H., and S. Newman, "Yokuts Western Mono Myths", *Anthropologyical Record*, V5:#1, Berkeley-Los Angeles, University of California Press, 1940.

Gayton, Anna H., "Twenty-Seven Chukchansi-Yokuts' Myths," JOURNAL OF AMERICAN FOLKLORE, 1944.

Gayton, Anna H., "Cultural-Environment Integration in Yokuts Life," SOUTHWESTERN JOURNAL OF ANTHROPOLOGY, 1946.

Gayton, A.H., "Yokuts and Western Mono Social Organization," AMERICAN ANTHROPOLIGIST, V. 47, pp. 409-426.

Gayton, A.H., "Yokuts-Mono Chiefs and Shamans", UNIVERSITY OF CALIFORNIA PUBLICATIONS IN AMERICAN ARCHAEOLOGY AND ETHNOLOGY, Vol. 24.

Gudde, Erwin Gustav, *California Place Names*: the Origin and Etymology of Current Geographical Names. rev. and enl. 3d ed., Berkeley: University of California Press, 1969.

Heizer, Robert F. and William C. Sturtevant, "A Collection of Ethnographical Articles on the California Indians", *Ballena Press Pubs., in Archaeology, Ethnology and History*, #7 and #15, Ramona, CA: Ballena Press, 1976.

Heizer, Robert F., *Handbook of North America Indians: California*, V. 8, Washington, D.C.: Smithsonian Institution, 1978.

Herzog, George, *The Yuman Musical Style & North American Indian Musical Style*, 1928.

Hoopes, Chad L., *Domesticate or Extermninate: California Indian Treaties Unratified and Made Secret in 1852*, Redwood Coast Publications, 1975.

Hoover Rench & Rench, *Historical Spots in California*, Palo Alto: Stanford University Press, 1966.

Hopkins, D., Source of material on pollen, 1972.

Hurtado, Albert L., *Indian Survival on the California Frontier*, New Haven: Yale University Press, 1988.

James, George Wharton, *Indian Basketry and How to Make Indian and Other Baskets*, 3d. ed., rev. and enl., New York: Henry Malcolm Publishing, 3rd edition, 1903.

Jennings, Jesse D., *Ancient North Americans*, San Francisco: W.H. Freeman, Co., 1983.

Kipp, Rev. William S., *Early Days of My Episcopate, The Journey of Rev. Kipp Through the Valley*, 1855.

Kopper, Philip, *The Smithsonian Book of North American Indians: Before the Coming of the Europeans,* editor-in-chief, Patricia Gallagher, 1986.

Kroeber, A. L., *Indian Myths of South Central California,* Berkeley: University Press, 1907.

Kroeber, Alfred L., *Karok Myths,* by E.W. Gifford, pub., with foreward by Theodore Kroeber; Folklorists Commentary by, Alan Dundes; Ed. Grace Bugalsiko, Berkeley: University of California Press, 1980.

Kroeber, Alfred L., *Handbook of the Indians of California,* Berkeley: California Book Co., 1953.

Kroeber, Alfred L., *Handbook of the Indians of California,* Washington D.C.: Smithsonian Insitiution, Bureau of American Ethnology, Bulletin 78, 1925.

Kroeber, Alfred L., *Indian Myths of South Central California,* Berkeley: University of California Press, 1907.

Kroeber, Alfred L., *The Yokuts Language of South Central California,* Berkeley: The University of California Press, 1907.

Laird, Carobeth, *Encounter With an Angry God: Recollections of My Life with John Peabody Harrington,* Banning, CA: Malki Museum Press, 1975..

Laird, Carobeth, "Two Chemehueivi Teaching Myths", *Journal of California Anthropology,* p. 18, 1975.

Latta, Frank, *California Indians Folklore, as told to F.F. Latta by Wah-no-Kot, Wah-hu-chah, Lee-ee and others.* Shafter, CA., 1936.

Latta, Frank, *Handbook of Yokuts Indians*, 1949, 2nd ed., rev. and enl., Santa Cruz, CA: Bear State Books, , 1977.

Librado, Fernando, and J.P. Harrington, *The Eye of the Flute*, Banning, CA: Morango Indian Reservation, Malki Museum Press, 1976.

Librado, Fernando, "The Eye of the Flute," *Library of Congress Catalog* #77-70777,Santa Barbara Museum of National History, Los Angeles: Westland Printing, 1977.

MacDonald, J.R., "The Maricopa Brea", *Los Angeles County Museum Quarterly*, Vol. 546, Fall 1967, pp 21-24.

Mayfield, Thomas Jefferson,*Tailholt Tales / by Frank F. Latta*, Santa Cruz, CA: Bear State Books, 1976.

Nettl, Bruno, "North American Indian Musical Styles," *Memories of the American Folklore Society*, Vol. 45, American Folklore Society, Philadelphia, 1954.

Pietroforte, Alfred, *Songs of the Yokuts and Piutes*, Healdsburg, CA: Nature Graph Publishing, , 1965.

Powers, Stephen, *Tribes of California*, reprint of 1877 publication by Government Print Office in Washington D.C., Berkeley: University of California Press, 1976.

Priestley, Herbert I., *Historical Political and Natural Description of California by Pedro Fages Soldier of Spain*, U.C. Berkeley Press, 1937. Ballena Pub. 1972.

Rawls, James J., *Indians of California: the Changing Image, ,* Norman: University of Oklahoma Press, 1984.

Riddle, Francis A. and William Olsen, *An Early Witt Site in the San Joaquin American Antiquity,* 1969.

Rogers, Barbara T., "Twenty-Seven Chukchansi-Yokuts Myths," JOURNAL OF AMERICAN FOLKLORE, 57 (225): pp. 190-207, 1944.

Sacks, Curt, *Wellsprings of Music,* New York: McGraw-Hill Book Company, 1965.

Small, Kathleen Edwards & Larry J. Smith, "Chapter II Indians War Tulare County & Kings County, Vol. I", 1926.

Smith, Wallace, *Garden of the Sun,*1939, 4th ed.reprint, Fresno: Hardison-A-1 Printers, 1960.

Sterling, M.W., "John Peabody Harrington,*The American Anthropologist,* 65 (1963): 370-381.

Steward, Julian H. "Alfred Louis Kroeber." *American Anthropologist* 63 (1961): 1038-59.

Stewart, George N., "Two Yokuts, Tradition-1908" & "A Yokuts Creation Myth-1906," *Journal of American Folklore,* 21: 237-239.

Sturtevant, William C., *Handbook of North American Indians,* Washington D.C.: Smithsonian Institution, 1978.

Thomason, D.L., "Cholama, The Beautiful One," *Cholame Valley History and Its Pioneer People*, John Lathaurahia, ed., San Luis Obispo-Parkfield: Tabula Rasa Press, 1988.

Tule River Indians Quarterly Bulletin of the Tulare County Historical Society, 68 (March 1966).

Washburn, Wilcomb E., "The American Indian Through the United States", 4 (1973).

Wilson, Norman and Arlene Towne, H.V. *Eastman Lake and Its Forgotten Frontiers*, Sacramento: U.S. Army Corps of Engineers Publication, Sacramento District, (1980).

Zigmond, Maurice L., "Kawaiisu Mythology, An Oral Tradition of South-Central California," *Ballena Anthropological Papers*, 18, 252 (1980).

INDEX

Addenda

A group of seventy professional archaeologists under the name TULARG (Tulare Lake Research Group) have joined together with the purpose of examining the possibilities of developing the old Lake Tulare as an early man site. It is now too late to develop the prime site all had believed to be the place of greatest opportunity for development as it has been thoroughly bulldozed for farming interest to create a holding pond. However, there is still much to be done.

The collections already assembled by owners of farm in the old lake bed area need to be examined and classified and some disposition made of them to a place where they can be viewed by the public and appreciated.

A Lost Opportunity

In "Reconnaissance of the Central San Joaquin Valley," published in American Antiquity in October 1941, Gordon W. Hewes reported the presence of large archaeological sites with great depth of deposit standing within a few hundred feet of one another.

Hewes concluded that:

"It is highly improbable that three extensive sites were simultaneously occupied by the number of primitive households required to accumulate such amounts of refuse; it is difficult to imagine how three large villages dependant upon hunting and gathering even in a rich slough region north of Tulare Lake could be supported at the same time. More likely there is a long history of shifting settlement by the same local group" (Ibid).

Stratigraphic excavations at large, deep archaeological sites like the three in the vicinity of Hanford could, Hewes suggested, produce materials belonging to different occupation periods. He expressed the hope that local central San Joaquin Valley institutions would take up the work. Unfortunately, nothing was ever done and a real opportunity for learning something about the region's human past was irretrievably lost, as the three sites were subsequently leveled. It can be guessed that digging into them may well have revealed a sequence of cultural phases similar to that documented 25 years later by excavations in the San Luis-Little Panoche area on the west side of the San Joaquin Valley (Olsen and Payen 1969:39-42).

Literature Cited

Hewes, Gordon W.
    1941   Reconnaissance of the Central San Joaquin Valley.
          American Antiquity 7(2):123-133.

Second TULARG Symposium!

The Tulare Lake Archaeological Research Group

Will present a symposium on Tulare Lake archaeology at the 1992 Annual Meeting of the Society for California Archaeology, April 24-26 in Pasadena, with Franklin Fenenga as Chairman. Seven papers, covering a wide range of topics, have been ''volunteered.''